The
Creative
Christian

Adrian B. Smith

BOOKS

Winchester, U.K.
New York, U.S.A.

First published by O Books, 2006
O Books is an imprint of John Hunt Publishing Ltd.,
The Bothy, Deershot Lodge, Park Lane, Ropley, Hants, SO24 0BE, UK
office1@o-books.net
www.o-books.net

Distribution in:

UK and Europe
Orca Book Services
orders@orcabookservices.co.uk
Tel: 01202 665432
Fax: 01202 666219
Int. code (44)

Far East (offices in Singapore,
Thailand, Hong Kong, Taiwan)
Pansing Distribution Pte Ltd
kemal@pansing.com
Tel: 65 6319 9939
Fax: 65 6462 5761

USA and Canada
NBN
custserv@nbnbooks.com
Tel: 1 800 462 6420
Fax: 1 800 338 4550

South Africa
Alternative Books
altbook@peterhyde.co.za
Tel: 021 447 5300
Fax: 021 447 1430

Australia and New Zealand
Brumby Books
sales@brumbybooks.com
Tel: 61 3 9761 5535
Fax: 61 3 9761 7095

Text copyright Adrian B. Smith 2006

Design: Jim Weaver

ISBN-13: 978 1 905047 75 8
ISBN-10: 1 905047 75 4

A CIP catalogue record for this book is available from the British Library.

Printed in the US by Maple Vail

Contents

Introduction

MOST of us were subjected to IQ tests as children. As adults we may have picked up one of those books which promise to test our *Intelligence Quotient*, to see what our chances are of being elected to Mensa! IQ tests were widely introduced into schools in the middle of the last century to determine the children's ability to solve logical problems. They were supposed to judge the level of our intelligence and so be an indication of our intellectual future. Their weakness was that they were a very left-brain, linear, logical measurement. They were assessing our level of rational thinking. They took no account of our intuitive, creative capacities nor of our feelings, our emotions.

Realising the limitation of the IQ measurement, Daniel Goleman pioneered work in the 1990s to show that our Emotional Intelligence, our EQ, was equally important. Assessing our 'feeling' ability took into account our awareness of our own and other people's emotions: our compassion, our empathy and our response to pleasure and pain. IQ and EQ are intimately connected. If the area of the brain with which we *feel* is damaged then we *think* less effectively.

Following this development, Danah Zohar and her husband Ian Marshall, both psychologists, have pioneered work in a third area of human life, which they felt was missing from the two previous areas, namely our Spiritual Intelligence, our SQ. In their book *Spiritual Intelligence* they describe it as 'the intelligence with which we address and solve problems of meaning and value, the intelligence with which we can place our actions and our lives in a wider, richer, meaning-giving context'. They go on to name it 'our ultimate intelligence'.

I beg to differ! I believe there is a fourth area, our Creative Intelligence, – CQ for short – which enables us as part of the human community, to create our future. Precisely because we are able to exercise our IQ, EQ and SQ we are freed and empowered as human creatures to determine the direction our evolution will take.

Creation is evolving. As water is to a fish – its element – so evolution is the element, the milieu, of our creativity. We are immersed in a Universe in flow towards its final fulfilment. Our species is evolving in consciousness. Each of us is evolving. We are in process of always becoming what we are meant to become.

Computers might be said to have an IQ in that they follow the rules fed into them and follow them without mistakes. Some animals have an EQ. They react in an appropriate manner to people and situations. But only a human being can exercise SQ or CQ because only a human being has the free will to plan and bring about our future and adapt to new circumstances. We create our own reality. We create our future.

While our level of IQ can be the result of our education and our EQ and SQ be largely determined by our upbringing, and unrelated to a formal education, our CQ, while based on and dependent upon the other three, will be greatly influenced by our culture and our religious experience.

In developing these thoughts on CQ I am doing so within a particular religious frame: that of the expressed SQ and CQ of Jesus of Nazareth.

There are certain qualities of CQ that need to be recognised and they will be explored in the first chapter. However, before we go further we need to list what is required of us if our creative intelligence is to be cultivated.

- It requires a development of our SQ. The word 'spiritual' comes from the Latin *spiritus* meaning breath, often referred to these days as our life energy. 'He's a person of spirit', we say. It is the non-physical part of our make up which includes our emotions, our courage, enthusiasm, determination: all essential ingredients of our creativity.

- It requires that we be people capable of a vision, who have at least our own sense of meaning and direction in life.
- It requires that we can envisage 'the big picture'; that we have the ability to see connections, to be able to stand back from the petty concerns of our everyday world and recognise the major trends moving humanity forward.
- It requires that we get excited at what we see! Identifying the positive and not being sucked into the negativity with which the media are always bombarding us.
- It requires that we are unafraid of the new, the not-yet-experienced: that we are prepared to take risks.
- It requires that we are consciously moving from being knowledge-driven to becoming wisdom-driven.
- It requires that we recognise the ways in which all humanity is being drawn towards a unity – a unity in its diversity.

Essential to the development of our CQ is our giving attention to our attitude. Having a right attitude in our relationships is the fundamental requirement for each of us to become the sort of person who is able to move humanity forward towards its ultimate point. Our attitude is the way our inside selves regard what is outside ourselves and it therefore governs our relationships: our relationships with other people, with ourselves, with our environment and with Ultimate Reality, however we understand this last. Each of these too will be developed later.

Recognising and correcting our relational attitude is also a process of healing, of becoming more whole, more effective 'artisans of a new humanity'.

'The attitude you should have is the one that Christ had', (Philippians 2:5).

Acknowledgements

I wish to thank the many people, participants in the workshops and seminars I have led, who have encouraged me to present in written form the thoughts we have shared together.

I am particularly grateful to those friends with expertise in theology and biblical studies who have enriched my text with their recommendations.

I also wish to express my gratitude to innumerable current authors whose insights have inspired me, particularly those whose books I mention.

PART ONE

The vision of Creative Intelligence

1 Our creative times

CONSCIOUSNESS is what gives birth to and upholds creation. Every creation begins with a thought. A thought is a form of energy. Add creativity to thought and you have imagination. Our nature is continually urging us to use the power of our creative imagination to expand our horizons. Imagination – imaging our creative thoughts – stimulates the transition from mere thoughts into action.

The 1960s is often regarded as the period when western culture took a leap forward to a new envisioning. It was the decade of the Hippies and Flower Power and student revolts. It saw the emergence of a plethora of ideas, practices, movements and new life-styles which were all bracketed together by the media under the umbrella name 'The New Age'. Many of its notions and practices, incidentally, were far from new but were a resurrecting of ancient cultural traditions.

But already in 1936 the French Jesuit, mystic and palaeontologist, Pierre Teilhard de Chardin wrote:

> We now have to accept it as proven that mankind has just entered into what is probably the most extensive period of transformation it has known since its birth.
>
> ... Today something is happening to the whole structure

of human consciousness: a fresh kind of life is beginning to appear. (*Science and Christ*)

This new consciousness is primarily an evolutionary, creative consciousness.

Any contemporary understanding of Creative Intelligence is dependent upon situating it in this present bursting forth of a new consciousness. Indeed, it is both the product of this new consciousness as well as the instrument of its further evolution.

Previous evolutionary stages – from the simple amoeba to plant life to animal life to human life – have come about by a natural, physical progression. This next step, forecast by Teilhard and others, is of a different nature. Precisely because it is an evolution in consciousness it can only come about through the agency of self-conscious creatures: through humanity deliberately taking this next step.

The new consciousness

What do we mean by a new consciousness? There is no neat definition available because it is not an objective 'thing' so much as an experience, an insight into a new awareness which is emerging. Consciousness itself can be viewed as a fundamental field. Like gravity or electromagnetic waves, its effects are readily experienced, but what it consists of and the actual mechanisms that give rise to it remain a mystery. Strangely, while it is the most objective of all phenomena, in that it is the one thing we can be sure we possess, consciousness is also the most subjective of all phenomena in that we can experience it in ourselves.

In a previous book (*A Reason for Living and Hoping*) I have devoted a chapter to the signs that abound in contemporary life in the western world which, taken together, indicate that a paradigm shift in human consciousness is coming about. Some have likened it to the great leap forward in human consciousness that took place among the predominant cultures between 600 and 300 BCE, named by the German existentialist Karl Jaspers, the 'Axial Period' because it was as if the evolution of human culture was taking a great turn on its axis and moving in a new direction. It was the period that produced the great sages: Gautama Siddhartha (the Buddha) and Patanjali in India, Lao Tzu and Confucius in China, Parmenides from Italy, Zoroaster in Iran, Pythagoras, Socrates, Plato, Aristotle from Greece, the sages of the Upanishads and the Hebrew Prophets. It was the period of the birth of the great religions: Zoroastrianism, Taoism, Confucianism, Jainism and Buddhism. Within Judaism it was a time of a forward leap in their understanding of a universal God and the period of compiling their great literary traditions: the Yahwistic, Elohistic, Deuteronic and Priestly. It was the era that saw the building of the Parthenon in Athens, the Lighthouse of Alexandria and other great monuments.

While contemporary writers are referring to our own times as another Axial period, increasingly more Christian authors too are recognising that we are entering a new shift in collective consciousness. I shall quote just one: the German Jesuit and Zen Master, Hugo Enomiya-Lassalle who wrote in 1988:

> (It) is certainly no secret today to the careful observer. Humanity stands at a turning point. We could even say that we find ourselves in the midst of a transformation of such dimensions that it occurs only once in millennia. (*Living in the New Consciousness*)

We are speaking of what Professor Ervin Laszlo, author and President of the Club of Budapest, called in his acceptance address of the Goi Peace Award in 2001: 'a holistic consciousness with an integrated vision of people, society, life and universe'. He went on to show how this was becoming evident at different levels of society. On the personal level it is the consciousness that socially and ecologically destructive behaviour is unacceptable. It is showing itself in the move towards simpler and more responsible lifestyles and consumer habits. Increasing numbers of people are changing their preferences, priorities, values and beliefs. At society level it is the realisation that other people, whether our next-door neighbour or in distant parts of the world, are an integral part of the human family. In the political sphere it means concern for the self-reliant development of grass-roots communities, while at the same time, all peoples are coming closer together through multi-cultural relationships and the electronic media to form a 'global village': the healthy aspects of globalisation. In our relationship to Nature and our environment, it is the conviction that we cannot do harm to the wider community of all living species on Earth without also doing harm to ourselves.

This is the paradigm in which our own creativity is being developed.

Society is propelled in this direction on account of the current shift from a Newtonian, analytical manner of thinking, by which the mind focuses on individual items, seeking to make sense of each part in itself, to what is named 'Systems Thinking'. Rather than the mind dividing up what it wishes to understand, the relational mind holds all elements together. It focuses on their relationships, seeking to make sense of things in context. While the analytical mind worked in either/or categories, sorting out the mutually exclusive, the relational mind enjoys the paradox of holding both/and in an inclusive context. It is this latter way of perceiving that gives the dynamic to creativity.

Creation

To speak meaningfully of creativity, we need to be clear about what we mean by creation. 'Creation' is a word used with a number of meanings. A fashion magazine will describe a new garment as the creation of a particular fashion house, introducing a new design. An artist or an author may use the word to refer to the product of the human imagination. 'Creation' is used in writing or speaking of the Universe including the world and all things in it, as in the exhortation: 'We must have respect for the whole of creation'. Scientists speak of the 'moment of creation' when referring to the Big Bang. (It would be less confusing if instead they spoke of the origin of the Universe.) But in this sense too there can be misunderstanding when creation is thought of as a once-and-for-all event at the beginning of time. Theologians speak of creation *ex nihilo*, out of nothing, in the sense that the Creator did not fashion the Universe out of already existing 'stuff' as did the 'creator' of the new garment.

The use of the word in this present work is with the understanding that the act of creation was not a one-time event but is the continuous act of causing and holding all things in existence. It is the perpetual action of the source of all energy which we name 'God'*.

In being creative of our future, some speak of our being co-creators with God. And so we are. But not in the sense that we are equal partners. God is the sole source of creative energy. We partner God in the framework of time and space, in that we give the divine, eternal plan day-to-day shape. We have the free will to co-operate with the divine plan or to frustrate or even oppose it. In this we are unlike any other creature. A dog can only act in a doggy fashion according to its instinct. It can therefore do no wrong, although what it does may displease us! A dog cannot cause evil. Its every action is in accord with the divine plan. Only human beings cause evil because only we have the free will to choose whether to promote or frustrate the evolutionary thrust of our species, of our planet.

Being creative

The creative mind reveals the following human characteristics. Originality: the ability to come up with ideas that are unique to it alone. Such ideas are arrived at through the ability to see things from a different angle, from another point of view, or even to take old concepts and re-arrange them in a different way. The creative mind can take a central idea and build on it in different directions, expanding and elaborating the original idea. With the activity of the Right Brain (the right side cortex) a situation can be grasped in its wholeness, its connectedness, rather than piece by piece. The creative mind envisages how things can be different.

Fundamental to our capacity to be creative is the exercise of the virtue of Hope. It is as important as Faith and Charity, with which it

---

* Throughout the book I shall refer to God with a capital H – Him, He, His – so as not to appear that I am giving God a masculine gender.

is grouped as a foundational virtue of Christian life. Yet it is the least respected of the three. It is called a virtue because it is a dimension of the spirit, not an intellectual judgement of future events. It is not simply a willingness to place a bet or to invest in something which stands a chance of succeeding. Nor is it the same as optimism. Without Hope we lose sight of life's horizon. It is an orientation of our spirit which gives us the will to live and continually to try new things. So many young people in the affluent western world are living without hope of a better future. 'The future of humanity lies in the hands of those who are strong enough to provide coming generations with reasons for living and hoping', declared the world's Catholic Bishops at the Second Vatican Council in 1965, (GS.31) echoing the words of Teilhard de Chardin.

Our future does not just happen. It is a human creation. It depends on the union of two forces. One is God's creative energy which pervades and sustains all creation (more of this in Chapter 9) always moving creation towards its final culmination, its Omega point. The other is our willing co-operation with this creative energy.

We find ourselves so locked in the present that it is not easy to open our minds to fresh horizons. It is a characteristic of adolescents that they dream dreams. They have ideals. They want to imitate their idol. They think they are going to right all wrongs, to change the world. Think back. Were these not our dreams once? Why have we allowed ourselves to become disillusioned? Why are we so reluctant to dream of what could be, to give our imagination a day out? Why do we let our present dictate our future?

The creative mind thinks big, dares to change, takes risks, is prepared to think differently, stretches itself, lets go, embraces a vision as deep as it is wide.

It is in our nature to explore, to go beyond what we believe are our boundaries. Why else climb mountains, sail round the world single-handed, go to the moon? Small children remind us of this urge. 'What if...?' they ask. It is as adults that we suppress it. We play safe.

If we view our future with fear it will affect our present-day lives. If we see our future as clear, attractive and hope-filled we will be enabled to regard the present in a different light. It is our need for security that causes us to maintain the past, the safe path, in such a way that we see our future as simply a continuation of the present. The creative mind views the future, not by comparison with the past, nor as the unfolding and development of the present, but as a new, original and bold conception. The quality of a creative idea is proportionate to how far it is removed from the normal. Its energy is derived from the attraction of the future, not from an impulse of the past. We are people on a journey.

This is beautifully expressed in a document of the Doctrine Commission of the Church of England on Christian Believing (1976): 'Christian life is an adventure, a voyage of discovery, a journey, sustained by faith and hope, towards a final and complete communion with the Love at the heart of all things'. This is equally applicable to the life of all humanity.

Journeying into the future

There are four characteristics of the journey of life. Each faces us with challenging questions. The first characteristic is an appreciation that life is indeed a journey. It cannot stop. There is no going back to some safe past where we were dependent on others. Our journey is one expression of our evolving Universe. We have to go with the flow, but be on the lookout perpetually for signposts along the way. So we set out with a purpose. There is a goal to be reached. We need to ask ourselves:

– Do I feel my life has a purpose at present? What is it?
– Or did I in the past? Does it need re-starting?
– To what extent does it influence my major decisions?

Secondly, it is a journey of growth. That means that as we travel we have to let go our false self, our ego, the facade we like to present to those around us. Our life's journey is from the self-centred baby to the final letting-go at the moment when we pass out of this world into a fuller life. A journey from the primacy of 'having' to the primacy of 'being'.

So we have to travel light, letting go of all unnecessary baggage. I recall seeing a film long ago about the Bushmen of the past in the Kalahari Desert of Southern Africa. The commentator said that they were the freest people in the world because all they possessed as nomads was what they could carry on their heads and in their two hands.

We need to ask ourselves:

> In what do I put my security?
> – in possessions?
> – in insurance policies?
> – in relationships?
> – in my employment, business?
> – in something greater than myself?
> – Am I owned by any of my possessions? Do they curtail my freedom?

When I took up residence in Zambia most of the houses in the up-market area of the cities had open-plan gardens. There was no need then for fences. When I left, fifteen years later, such was the level of burglaries that every house was surrounded by high walls and security gates. But much worse, once darkness fell, always around 6.00 pm, no one dared to leave their premises unoccupied. The evening social life, with its parties, cinemas and theatres died a death. People had become the slaves of their possessions. With their possessions dictating their lives, the owners had become dehumanised.

Thirdly, our journey has a community dimension. All through life we need others for our physical, psychological and spiritual needs. We only learn to love by our experience of being loved.

We depend upon others we meet along the way. Am I able to receive from others? Am I able to acknowledge my dependence upon others?

We travel with others.

> – Am I free to choose what company I keep?
> – Do some people restrict my personal freedom?
> – Am I a slave to any persons? Or to their opinions of me?

– How much do I depend upon the support of like-minded people?
– Do I feel free to share myself, my possessions with others?
– Are there people whose company makes me buzz with energy?
– Do I allow others to love me?

We grow through service to others.
Then finally there is the route itself.

– Am I stuck in a rut?
– Am I open to change?
– Am I free enough to change to what I see as a route more conducive to growth?

Then what is stopping me?
I am part of the creative act of the Universe.
Can I make a difference? Yes, by following the example of one who has already done so. He called himself 'The Way'.

2 The SQ of Jesus of Nazareth

I T was a baking-hot sultry day in Israel when I chose to walk along the western edge of the Sea of Galilee from North to South. By the afternoon I was sweating profusely. Finding a secluded spot I stripped and plunged into the refreshing water of the lake. As I floated on my back, cooling myself, it dawned on me that others must have done the same in these waters from time immemorial. That two thousand years ago one, Jesus, and a band of followers must also have experienced the heat and humidity and taken the chance to cool off just as I was doing.

How was it, I mused, that the vision of a man of humble background from Galilee, a despised and deprived area of this Middle East country, could have made such an impact on world history and extended his influence right up to our present day? For the most part, his dream of how the world might be was addressed not to the religious or political leaders and the influential but to peasants.

This refreshing dip brought home to me, more than anything I had read in the gospels, just how human Jesus was. Like me, he and his companions must have felt the need to stop for a drink to quench their thirst – except with this difference that their source of water would have been a well: mine was a plastic bottle!

I had to rethink my previous ideas about this unique man who appeared on the human stage for such a brief period two thousand years ago, yet who still influences the minds of over a billion people world-wide today.

As a child I was brought up to believe in a Jesus who was 'the only-begotten Son of God', the Second Person of the Blessed Trinity. The emphasis was on his divinity, not on his humanity.

The balance between Jesus as God and Jesus as man has been tipping from one to the other since the earliest days of the Church. Once the story of Jesus had been taken by Paul and his followers into the Greek cultural world of Asia Minor, the Good News *of* Jesus became the Good News *about* Jesus. The message was eclipsed by the mystery of the messenger. Endless philosophical arguments took place as to who Jesus actually was. Some, who were labelled the Docetists, spoke of his being God but not truly man: he only had the appearance of man, his humanity being a veil for his divinity. Consequently, his sufferings and his death were apparent rather than real. Others (like the Adoptionists) believed that Jesus began by being completely human but was raised to the exalted position of divine. Bishop Apollinaris (c.310-c.390) taught that in Jesus the physical living organism was human while his spirit was divine. He defended the absolute Godhead of the Son and the true Deity of Jesus' person. Nestorius (d.250) was accused of teaching that there are two persons in Jesus, the divine person of the Word and the human person born of Mary.

Thus they continued to argue. All very philosophical! Since such opposing views were causing factions in the Church they were a threat to the unity of the Holy Roman Empire. The Emperor Constantine decided to step in. He called the bishops together for a Council in Nicaea in 325. From this we have the Nicene Creed recited by Christians down to this day.

Even this was not the final word, and it was not until the Council of Chalcedon (451) that the Church produced a definition of Jesus the Christ which has remained authoritative for all Western Churches, Catholic and Reformed, and for the Orthodox Churches of the East. Frances Young (*The Making of the Creeds*) comments on this:

> The Definition is seen as a political compromise which does not present any coherent christology, rather a paradox. This

leaves it open to challenge, and such challenges often go further than the charge of incoherence, suggesting that the problems arise from 'outdated substance language'. People ... suggest that we should start all over again and reject the formulations agreed in a completely different cultural and philosophical setting.

Most Christians in the West are unaware that so great was the controversy about the nature of Jesus the Christ at the Council of Chalcedon that it split the Christian Church into three streams that are with us still: the Nestorians in Persia and China, the Coptics in Egypt and Ethiopia and all others in the rest of the world.

One cannot help reflecting that during those first four centuries of argument and counter-argument about whether or how much Jesus was God and man, and how to explain the 'two natures in one person', what was never questioned was who or what God is. The bishops presumed on a theistic understanding of a God whom they were quite sure they knew all about! Their argument ran: 'We know about God. We believe Jesus is God the Son. Therefore Jesus must have all the attributes of God'. But this is topsy-turvy. We do not know all about God. We conjecture about God from what we know about ourselves and supremely from the little we know about Jesus whom St Paul calls: 'The visible image of the invisible God' (Colossians 1:15).

Consequently in the centuries that followed these Councils there was more emphasis on the divinity of Jesus than on his humanity. For the last few decades the balance has been tipping the other way. Authors are searching Scripture and the writings of contemporary historians to try to discover the 'real', historical Jesus, his authentic words and actions.

How we conceive of Jesus gives a shape to our Christian life. The most widespread image among believers today is of Jesus who as Son of God came down to Earth to die for the sins of the world and so save all humanity from the wrath of God. To benefit from this salvation requires our belief. So belief in Jesus and what we know of his life is uppermost. The primary dynamic of the Christian life of people with this understanding is Faith.

There are a lesser number of believers who understand Jesus primarily as a teacher: he came to show us 'The Way' to a new life. The spiritual dynamic of these Christians is morality: to follow the moral code Jesus gave us. But are Faith or Morality really the essence of Jesus' mission? Are they what a Christian life is all about? We shall see later that the heart of Jesus' vision – so his message – was about an evolution in our relationships.

Our sources

That Jesus has been a mysterious person from the earliest days of Christianity is not so surprising when we consider that no such thing as a biography of Jesus exists. What we do have is a collection of writings – gospels and letters – in which the author of each presented a particular aspect of the life and message of Jesus which he thought was appropriate for announcing the Good News to his particular readership. Each author had his own subjective view and this depended largely upon his own source of information. So there has never been just one official document about Jesus. The Gospels of Mark, Luke and Matthew were not written during the life of Jesus. It cannot even be taken for granted that the authors of any of the above three gospels, which we name the Synoptic (meaning 'seen together') Gospels because of their similarity, was a close associate of Jesus. But all three did belong to the time of the apostles. The Gospel named John was written much later, around 100 CE. The majority of scholars today recognise that there is no certainty about its author. It was most probably written by one of the members of the community founded by the one who is always referred to as 'the disciple whom Jesus loved'.

The Gospel of John presents a highly evolved theology of Jesus. The understanding of Jesus as the Christ and the theology of his divinity we owe to John's Gospel and to the letters of St Paul. Written for a non-Jewish readership, the emphasis is on the supernatural character of Jesus. Jesus as 'the Word' is clearly identified as God (John 1:1), although none of the Gospel writers record Jesus himself as saying he was God (with one ambiguous exception: Mark 14:61-62). The idea that a man could be a god was utterly alien to Judaism.

The three truths, which are fundamental to Christianity as it is presented today, are the Incarnation (that God sent his Son to Earth for our salvation), the Trinity (expressed as three persons in one God) and Redemption (that we are saved from God's wrath by the death of Jesus as a sacrifice and the shedding of his blood). We owe the first two beliefs to John's Gospel. The development of a doctrine of the Trinity (the word 'Trinity' appears nowhere in the Bible) derives from John's report of Jesus speaking of the oneness of himself with the Father (John 10:30) and by John assigning a personal status to the Holy Spirit (John 14:16-17).

It is from John's Gospel too (but also from the post-Pauline letters of Colossians and Hebrews) that is born the doctrine of the Incarnation, not found in the Synoptic Gospels. (Both Matthew and Luke speak of the birth of Jesus but not as one come down from Heaven.) In the prologue to John's Gospel is mentioned the pre-existence of Jesus as the Christ and elsewhere that Jesus was 'sent' into the world by God (John 3:17). One may conjecture that the author wrote under Greek influence: the myth of a god descending to Earth.

A non-mythical way by which one might understand the Incarnation – a way more in keeping with contemporary thinking – is this. Jesus introduced us by his own manner of life to a new way of perceiving God. First, as a presence in all creation by recognizing the divinity of each human being with whom he came into contact. Secondly, as unconditional love, mirrored in the way we humans love. In this sense Jesus brought God down to Earth, into daily life: he incarnated (made human) this perception of God. By his own perceiving and acting upon this insight, it became a reality in him. God became a reality in him. God was manifest in him. He was the personification of God's unconditional love. He incarnated God.

Paul presents quite another aspect of Jesus. The scholarly publication *The Oxford Dictionary of the Christian Church* speaks of Paul as 'the creator of the whole doctrine and ecclesiastical system presupposed in his epistles'. Paul is widely held by scholars today as the real founder of the Christian religion and its institutions as we know it in the West today. It is Paul who emphasises Jesus as the universal Redeemer.

We need to keep in mind that most of the letters attributed to Paul are the earliest texts of the New Testament and that he himself was not an eye-witness to the life of Jesus but learnt about Jesus from those that were (I Corinthians 15:3). Paul's chief interest in the life of Jesus was his crucifixion and this as the supreme event by which Jesus redeemed the world. Paul wrote to the community in Corinth: 'The message of Christ's death on the cross is nonsense to those who are being lost; but for those who are being saved it is God's power' (I Corinthians 1:18).

The gospels were written later, greatly under the influence of Paul's preaching. All four give detailed descriptions of Jesus' suffering and death. They were not written in the order in which we find them in our Bibles. Scholars are still undecided about the order in which they were written but the most universally accepted view is that Mark was the earliest and was written some thirty-five years after the crucifixion. Luke's came next, borrowing heavily from Mark and then came Matthew who borrowed from both. It is to these three, the Synoptics, that we look to learn about the humanity of Jesus and also of his vision for the world which we will develop in the next chapter. All three present Jesus as a teacher who, through his obedience to God in following what he understood to be his call, is raised up to be the Christ. Yet even among themselves they present a different Jesus: that aspect of his character each felt to be the best to put across the message to his readers.

Excavating the myth of Jesus

Increasingly over the last two centuries, scholars have been digging beneath the surface of the gospels to discover what we can factually know about Jesus the man and what is devout myth that grew up about him in the early decades of the Christian community. (To name any biblical account as a myth is not to deny its theological truth. It is to say that there is no proof of its factual or historical truth.)

Until the Council of Nicaea (325) there were many written records about Jesus circulating among the Christian communities. We now know of two documents which preceded the four canonical gospels. One is referred to as 'Q' (from the German *Quelle* meaning 'source') which was the source of information for the gospels of Matthew and Luke. The other is the Gospel of Thomas discovered in 1945. What is significant is that both say next to nothing about the life, death and resurrection of Jesus. They relate what was, for those first Christians, the most important feature of Jesus' life: what he said. This suggests that in those early years of the communities of 'The Way' it was the teaching of Jesus, not his crucifixion which was central. Jesus of Nazareth was primarily a teacher of wisdom.

If we are really to understand what Jesus was about, we have to excavate beneath all the myths that have grown up about him, such as his birth in Bethlehem, the wise men and the star, the flight to Egypt, the number of apostles being twelve and many of the miracles which were used later as proofs of his divinity, the accounts of his trials, the empty tomb, the resurrection appearances.

Delving beneath these we find that Jesus was primarily a teacher, a sage. This was how his contemporaries understood him (John 3:2). Over and over again he is addressed as 'teacher', altogether forty-three times in the four gospels. What he taught was mostly in short aphorisms (sound-bites) and parables, in the Jewish wisdom tradition, as in the books of Proverbs, Job, Ecclesiastes. It was the teaching of Jesus which fired the early Christians. Jesus was crucified – and crucifixions were only too common in his time – because of what he taught, which was a threat to the religious leaders.

In the tradition of the Hebrew sages, he was more concerned to improve the life of his people in their daily trials and problems, than to teach what we would call 'religion'. He said very little about God because his audience was a believing people who did not need to be persuaded about God. But the little he did say – calling God *Abba,* Father – was absolutely revolutionary. He said almost nothing about worship. He taught no abstract doctrine but about daily life and of the way in which people should relate to one another. Like any good teacher, he did not simply impart information, he wanted to help people to grow and mature. He urged people to take responsibility for their lives: to build a house on firm rock, not on sand. As with the great religions of his time, he was more concerned with how people behaved than in what they believed.

That it was Jesus' death that bought the forgiveness of God was a much later doctrine. Nothing could have been further from his mind as his famous parable of the Prodigal Son, in which Jesus compares the father with God, reveals. This and other parables and events (Matthew 18:12,23. Mark 2:1. Luke 7:36, 19:1, 23:29 and John 8:1, 21:15) reveal that it is God's unconditional love that forgives without any need of sacrifice or atonement or for a blood-price to be paid. Jesus' saving action was not in making reparation on our behalf for a past Fall, but in giving us a vision of how the future could be. 'I must preach the Good News of the Kingdom in other towns also because that is what God sent me to do' (Luke 4:43).

How did Jesus' vision develop?

Our concern here is about the SQ, the level of Spiritual Intelligence of Jesus, which gave rise to his creativity, expressed as a vision of what the world could be like for humanity.

In what lay the roots of his vision? What were the sources from which he drew, to propose to people a world of harmony, for which he used the metaphor 'The Kingdom of God'?

Jesus the Jew

Important in understanding the SQ of Jesus is to recognise what we know of his cultural background. He was brought up in the traditions and culture of the Middle East.

Along with his contemporaries, he believed he lived on a flat Earth, he knew nothing of what was beyond the Mediterranean Sea. He would only have had the medical knowledge of his time, not knowing about epilepsy as we do but believing that mental disorder was caused by evil spirits. His Father God had an abode above the clouds and in the depth of the Earth was *sheol* or *gehenna*.

We must be emphatically clear that Jesus was deeply Jewish. His ancestry was Jewish, his culture Jewish, his family were Jewish, his followers were all Jews, his audience was Jewish, Paul and all the authors of the New Testament (except Luke) were Jews. He went to a Jewish school, learned to pray the psalms and studied Jewish history. Jesus was steeped in the Jewish religious tradition. Although he had a great appreciation of Jewish law – 'Do not think that I have come to do away with the Law of Moses' (Matthew 5:17-19) – when he finds a human need is disregarded in favour of right observance of the law, he gives priority to the former. He often healed on the Sabbath thus breaking the law. 'The Sabbath was made for the good of man: man was not made for the Sabbath' (Mark 2:27). He understood his mission was to challenge the social and religious values of his own people. It never occurred to him to found a new religion. In his manner of thinking Jesus remained Jewish.*

His introduction to the Hebrew Scriptures would have played a large part in his religious formation. These, coupled with the weekly instruction he received with the other boys of the village in his local synagogue plus the rituals that were celebrated, mostly at home, weekly and annually, would have made him very aware of being one of God's special elect, the Chosen People, to whom God had promised a Messiah. He would have learnt his people's history, how they came to understand more deeply God's special providence for the Jews, how God expressed His preference for them through His actions on their behalf.

Many beliefs of his people had been assumed into Hebrew theology from the Zoroastrian religion during the Jews' forty-eight years in exile in Babylon. Such beliefs as two principal forces in cosmic conflict for control of the world, the idea of angels, of a personal devil and accompanying demons, the recording of our deeds in a Book of Life, the separation of the body and soul at death, a general resurrection

---

* Lack of this awareness has been largely responsible for two millennia of the anti-Semitic attitude of Christians. When they read in the Gospel of John that 'the Jews' challenged Jesus and in the end had him put to death, they are unaware that it was not his own people but only a small powerful elite among the religious leaders, collaborating with the Romans, who felt threatened by him and so plotted his execution.

and universal judgement with an after-life of reward or punishment and the vision of a messianic figure who would introduce a new age by overcoming the powers of evil. (Many of these beliefs have passed into Christian faith down to this day.)

Another factor to have influenced Jesus' religious thought was the apocalyptic ideas of his contemporaries. We are familiar with the last book of the Bible, the Book of Revelation, in some bibles called the Apocalypse. Apocalyptic literature was very widespread among the Jews of Jesus' time offering visions and revelations of the future. It was a religious outlook which contrasted the present time of suffering with a new age which would be joyful and eternal. Such a time would suddenly break in from outside by divine intervention. Although Mark (12 times), Matthew (24 times) and Luke (21 times) put such prophecies in the mouth of Jesus, we might suspect that many were inserted by the gospel writers after the fall of Jerusalem to the Roman army in 70 CE, to give their people hope of a better future.

Such apocalyptic warnings of an imminent 'end-time' about to break through dramatically were out of keeping with what Jesus actually taught. He said the Kingdom of God would come about quietly and unobtrusively. 'The Kingdom of God does not come in such a way as to be seen. No one will say "Look, here it is!" or "There it is!" because the Kingdom of God is within you' (Luke 17:20-21). The spread of the Kingdom would be like leaven working its way slowly through the dough. The Kingdom would spread, not through the exercise of force from above but from the grass-roots as more and more people began to live by the values he lived.

Jesus' idea of God

The Hebrew scriptures are not theology books telling us of the nature of God. They are all about God relating to, and His actions on behalf of, His Chosen People. A Jewish boy is brought up in this awareness of and closeness to God, albeit a transcendent God.

We each of us from childhood built up an idea *about* God to which a number of factors contributed. The most significant of these was our relationship with our parents, and perceiving the way in which they related to Someone even greater than they. From the few accounts we have, we gain the impression that Jesus' mother Mary was a very spiritual person, and biographers like to think it was under her influence that her son's spirituality grew. The religious education of sons was the sacred responsibility of the father, so it was most probably from Joseph (who is called 'just') that his thinking of God as a loving father originated. Joseph was his first '*Abba*'. It is traditionally supposed that Joseph died while Jesus was still an adolescent because no mention is made of him after the incident in the Jerusalem Temple when Jesus was twelve years old. Did Jesus' closeness to God replace the father of his boyhood? God was a presence for him 'as if a father'. Curiously, there is only one mention in the gospel of his declaring his love for the Father (John 14:31).

To have a healthy and balanced image of and relationship to God depends largely upon our own self-image, our sense of self-worth. We know nothing about Jesus' family life in Nazareth except that he must have grown up in the company of his four brothers and at least two sisters (Mark 3:32 and 6:3). There are three explanations offered for this reference to his siblings. The first is that the words 'brother' and 'sister' are used loosely. When I lived in Zambia I learned that the people, lacking the concerns for genealogy that we have in the West, made less distinction of exact relationships within extended families. Those we would name cousins were referred to as brothers and sisters. This might have been equally applicable in rural Galilee. A second explanation is that they were in fact blood brothers and sisters. The Church has problems with this understanding because it puts in question the doctrine of Mary's virginity. A third theory is that Joseph's first wife, who bore him sons and daughters, died and that in middle age he married the young Mary. Traditional art has always depicted Joseph as elderly beside the youthful Mary. She gave him one son, Jesus. Had the brothers James, Joseph, Jude and Simon been the sons of Mary would they not have taken their mother under their protection after the crucifixion? As it was, Jesus entrusted her to a non-family member, John, a disciple (John 19:27).

While we can conjecture that his childhood and adolescence must have built the character that we have come to know in the last years of his life, there can have been nothing outstanding about him as a boy. 'Not even his brothers believed in him' (John 7:5). Certainly nothing out of the usual was recognised by his village playmates at the time. When he returned to Nazareth years later as an itinerant preacher his contemporaries were indignant. 'He taught in the synagogue, and those who heard him were amazed. "Where did he get such wisdom?" they asked. "And these miraculous powers? Isn't he the carpenter's son? Isn't Mary his mother, and aren't James, Joseph, Simon and Jude his brothers? Aren't all his sisters living here? Where did he get all this?" And so they rejected him' (Matthew 13:54-57). From the way in which he turned questions back on his interrogators, from his verbal gifts of employing imaginative and poetic language, from his skill in debate, Jesus was clearly exceptionally intelligent. In today's terms he was a highly developed left-brain and right-brain thinker.

We need to distinguish at this point the two ways in which we come to knowledge. The first we call 'Rational Knowledge'. This is knowledge *about* something or someone. It is information. We receive it from outside ourselves, through one or more of our five senses of sight, touch, hearing, smell and taste. Since it comes from without, from the knowledge and experience of others, it is always second-hand. The other way of knowing is by direct knowledge, often referred to as 'Intuitive Knowledge'. We call the first Rational Knowledge because the mind, receiving it from outside, rationalises the information, catalogues it and stores it away with previous knowledge to be drawn upon later. Intuitive Knowledge, on the other hand, is quite instantaneous and can be a sudden insight or inspiration, often coming to us in an unlikely moment. On rare occasions it can come to one in a dream, as 'voices' or even as an apparition. As experiences they have no value in themselves until we have interpreted them. But our interpretation is inevitably made in the context of our culture, our rational knowledge, our belief system, our values and our previous experience.

What is evident from the gospels is that in adulthood Jesus was gifted with a high degree – the highest possible degree – of Intuitive Knowledge. What shone through him was not a knowledge *about*

God as much as a direct experience *of* God. How did this come about? He must at some point (before or after his baptism by John) have had an enlightening experience. These are not uncommon. They are spoken of more widely today. They are experienced by people of all religious convictions or none. Abraham Maslow speaks of a 'peak experience' when one enters a not-ordinary state of consciousness and breaks through to a reality beyond material reality, to an insight that there is more than the senses can know. This is not a leap into another realm, out of this world. It is the experience that there is a deeper dimension here, all around us. Often the experience produces a feeling of complete union with people, with nature. Everything shines bright, is charged with energy and power. It is an experience of the Spirit. We know of many in Jewish history who had such mystical experiences (Abraham, Jacob, Moses, Elijah, to name a few) and in our New Testament we read of Mary's angel and Joseph's dreams, of the apostles receiving messages from or even seeing angels. Paul had his conversion vision. It is not surprising that Jesus had visions: seeing Heaven opened and the Spirit coming down on him like a dove as he was baptised (Mark 1:10) and of the Devil during his retreat in the desert (Matthew 4:3). There are three reports of his hearing the voice of God: at his baptism in the Jordan (Matthew 3:17), on Mount Tabor during the event we call the Transfiguration (Matthew 17:5) and on one occasion John records Jesus being praised by God (John 12:28-29). When Jesus is challenged by the Jewish authorities he declares:

'You have never heard His voice or seen His face' (John 5:37) which might imply that Jesus did have that experience. He stood in the mystic tradition.

A spiritual phenomenon or experience is one thing, but to engage with it, to allow it to impact upon our lives, the inexpressible has to be interpreted and the interpretation will always be according to our culture, our education, as I have already said. Our interpretation of a spiritual experience is based upon our faith, our beliefs. Jesus' interpretation of his inner experience of the Divine could only be within the framework of his Jewish upbringing.

Luke has a neat expression with which he rounds off his two chapters on the birth and boyhood of Jesus: 'Jesus grew both in body and in wisdom, gaining favour with God and men' (Luke 2:52). Can we say of him, in today's terminology, that he grew in unity consciousness so that two decades later he could claim: 'The Father and I are one' (John 10:30)? He also grew in an understanding of his mission, his purpose in life, though this was not to be confirmed and launched upon until some 20 years later.

The prayer of Jesus

Geza Vermes, the Jewish Biblical scholar, once Catholic priest, has written: 'Prayer is the most direct source disclosing a person's attitude and feelings towards God' (*The Changing Faces of Jesus*). In the case of Jesus, the first thing his praying to his Father reveals, as do a number of things he is quoted as having said (e.g. 'The Father is greater than I' John 14:28), is that he did not consider himself to be God. Like us, he felt the human need to draw his moral strength from an intimacy with God. He experienced what we are calling 'unity consciousness' with the Divine.

Was that moral strength being sapped along with his physical strength as he was dying on the cross? During those hours he seems to have lost his sense of unity with the Divine. 'Jesus cried out with a loud shout: "*Eloi, Eloi, lama sabachthani?*" which means: "My God, my God, why have you abandoned me?"' (Mark 15:34). This is the only prayer of Jesus in which God is not addressed as Father.

It is curious to notice that although the gospels frequently locate Jesus in synagogues – as a good Jew he would have been a weekly attender – they never speak of him as going there to pray. We know he went up to the Temple in Jerusalem during the Passover pilgrimage, but the gospels never mention that he participated in sacrificial worship.

With the exception of his shared prayer with his friends following the Last Supper (John 17) and what we call the 'Lord's Prayer', which was given to a group as an instruction on how to word their prayer, and occasional voiced ejaculatory prayers (e.g. Matthew 26:27, Mark 14:36, 15:34, John 11:41, 12:27) he is usually depicted as practising very private prayer. This is either in solitude or at least well away from people. As well as his prayer on a mountain, he is reported as praying in the desert (Matthew 4:1) and 'He would go away to lonely places where he prayed' (Luke 5:16), and in a garden away from his disciples: 'Then he went off from them about the distance of a stone's throw and knelt down and prayed' (Luke 22:41).

Furthermore, in his advice to others on prayer, he insists on privacy, 'When you pray, go to your room, close the door, and pray to your Father who is in secret. And your Father, who sees in secret, will reward you'. He then goes on, as a preface to teaching the Lord's Prayer: 'When you pray do not use a lot of meaningless words, as the pagans do, who think that God will hear them because their prayers are long. Do not be like them. Your Father already knows what you need before you ask Him' (Matthew 6:6-8). He surely followed his own advice! Jesus would have taken part in the Jewish liturgy, the community worship, but, like so many of us, felt another need. All the above passages seem to indicate that Jesus' own prayer was that of meditation, which in western asceticism we call 'contemplation'.

Jesus' higher consciousness

Jesus was a contemplative, a mystic. Putting together the evidence we have – the profundity of what he said, his complete lack of self-concern and the 'miraculous' powers he was able to draw upon – it is apparent that he was a totally fulfilled, enlightened human being. As Peter said to Cornelius and his family: 'You know about Jesus of Nazareth and how God poured out on him the Holy Spirit and power', (Acts 10:38).

For centuries Christians have been taught that this power, manifested in physical and spiritual healing, in multiplying material objects, in resuscitating 'dead' people, in defying the elements, issued from the fact that he was divine, in the Nicene sense of being 'God made man'. They were paraded, in fact, as proof of his divinity.

Today, we in the West, know more about the super-normal powers – 'siddhis' as they are called in the East – exercised by highly enlightened human beings in India and we can witness these people performing the very same 'miracles'. We are therefore better placed to attribute the super-normal powers exercised by Jesus, not as unique to him because he was God, but as the fruit of his being a fully enlightened person living in the highest state of consciousness. The exercise of these powers is not beyond the realms of our human nature, it is just that most of us have not yet evolved to that level of consciousness. But Jesus promised that one day we would: 'I am telling you the truth: whoever believes in me will do what I do – yes, he will do even greater things' (John 14:12).

One feature of the higher levels of consciousness which Jesus evidently enjoyed, is a sense of timelessness. Such mystics live in the eternal NOW of God. His saying 'Before Abraham was, I AM' (John 8:58) indicates his freedom from the dictates of time. Being free of this constraint, according to three thousand year old Vedic wisdom, leads to inner freedom. In so many ways Jesus manifests his personal freedom: free to live his true reality, free of the inhibitions induced by the fears that we suffer, free right up to his accepting death: 'Bowing his head, he gave up his spirit' (John 19:30). Only one living in the highest state of consciousness can experience that total unity with the Divine which Jesus experienced and manifested.

A new human form

It would seem that beyond understanding his mission as that of introducing a new world order, he understood himself to be the new human being that was required to make this new order a reality. In an evolutionary perspective, humanity is continually growing in consciousness. Jesus would appear to be one of the milestones in this evolution, breaking through on humanity's behalf into a more perfect form of humanity, a humanity free of any inner coercion.

The very first creatures we can recognise as being human – those primates which became capable of a self-reflective consciousness – would be the first to have the potential to experience an other-worldly or divine presence in creation, the existence of a greater Other. In this sense we can say they were the first incarnation (that is, in human flesh) of the Divine. The Jesus event a million or more years later, was the achievement of humanity reaching its incarnational maturity. In Jesus was enfleshed the divine idea of the perfect human person. This is why St Paul speaks of Jesus as the new Adam. 'The first man, Adam, was created a living being, but the last Adam is the life-giving Spirit.... The first Adam made of earth came from the earth; the second Adam came from heaven' (I Corinthians 15:45, 47) and 'He is the first-born son, superior to all created things' (Colossians 1:15).

Put all this together and it gives us a glimpse of the spiritual dimension of Jesus, his SQ, which gave birth to his vision of what a new world order might be like, the fruit of his creativity, his CQ.

3   The CQ of Jesus of Nazareth

O UR creativity is the fruit of the interaction between our IQ, our EQ and our SQ. In this chapter we will, in broad strokes only, because space does not allow for more, look at the vision created by the mind of Jesus.

His vision was of a new way for humanity to live in harmony: in harmony with each other and so in harmony with the Divine. But it was a vision that he related only to the situation of his own people, the Jewish race. 'I have been sent only to those lost sheep, the people of Israel', he declared (Matthew 15:24). He even instructed his disciples: 'Do not go to any Gentile territory and do not enter any Samaritan towns. Instead, you are to go to those lost sheep, the people of Israel' (Matthew 10:5-6). This is the reason why he described his vision of how the world might be in the metaphoric term of 'The Kingdom of God'. In using this expression he was partially addressing the contemporary expectations of his compatriots who were longing for, indeed expecting, a saviour to arise in their country to rid them of the Roman occupation of their land and restore the glorious days of the Kingdom of David. Many of his audience understood his words in just this way (Mark 11:10). I say 'partially' because the kingdom of which Jesus spoke was not of an earthly kind but of a manner of living ordained by interior spiritual power rather than by external human-controlled power.

Precisely because of its inner, spiritual dimension, his vision is in fact applicable to the whole of humanity, transcending all races and cultures. A Jew, Sholem Ash, speaks of Jesus in these words:

> Jesus Christ is the outstanding personality of all time. ... No other teacher – Jewish, Christian, Buddhist, Mohammedan – is still a teacher whose teaching is such a guidepost for the world we live in. Other teachers may have something basic for an Oriental, an Arab or an Occidental; but every act and word of Jesus has value for all of us. He became the Light of the World. Why shouldn't I, a Jew, be proud of that. (Cited by Frank Mead in *The Encyclopedia of Religious Quotations.*)

The potential of Jesus' vision lies in the very nature of the human person understood as being destined for unity with the Divine. It was a message about the here and now, not a message about the after-life, even though the gospel of Matthew has Jesus speak of the 'Kingdom of Heaven' in places where Mark and Luke use the expression 'Kingdom of God'. (Matthew's reason for this is that he was writing for Jews who had become Christians and they still held God in such awe that they would not even mention His name. Similarly in English we might say 'Heaven help us', 'Heaven forbid' or 'Heaven knows'.)*

Jesus embodies the new person

Jesus' Good News was of a new world order emerging, not a possibility only, but as actually becoming a reality through his very person. How could he claim that? Such was his integrity and his overpowering sense of living in union with the Divine that he was able to live by the very values he preached. He was the living embodiment of the 'new person', the 'new creation'. His words were no more than an explanation of the values by which he lived.

---

* I have written extensively about the mystery, the dimensions and the different expressions of 'The Kingdom of God' in *A Reason for Living and Hoping.*

His vision was not a mere dream of what might be in the future. He perceived it as a present reality, a potential to be lived. It was not a fairy-tale with 'let's pretend' or 'let's do as if'. His manner of living and relating said: 'actualise it by living it'. He showed any who had 'the eyes to see' that the Kingdom way of relating is present and just waiting to be manifest. Two millennia later Mahatma Gandhi has given us the same message: 'Be the change you want to see in the world'. Jesus lived the change. He was the change. Change happened.

This was transparent to the unsophisticated folk, the peasants of Galilee. They recognised in him an authority different from their religious leaders: 'The crowd was amazed at what he taught. He wasn't like the teachers of the Law: instead he taught with authority' (Matthew 7:28-29). His authority did not come from election to a religious position nor from the affirmation of the Scribes, who were the official interpreters of the Law of Moses. While their authority was a legal, institutional authority, that of Jesus derived from his personal charisma: it lay in the power of his message. 'They were all well impressed with him and marvelled at the eloquent words that he spoke' (Luke 4:22).

Yet he was extremely reserved in speaking about himself (Luke 10:22). He never claimed to be omnipotent (Mark 6:5) nor omniscient (Matthew 24:36) nor even that he was completely good (Luke 18:19). He never spoke of himself as a god or equal with his God. 'I am going to the Father: for he is greater than I' (John 14:28).

He proclaimed: 'I was born and came into this world for this one purpose, to speak about the truth' (John 18:37) and on another occasion: 'I must preach the Good News of the Kingdom of God in other towns also, because that is what God sent me to do' (Luke 4:43). His single-mindedness shone through him.

Envisaging a different way of living and relating, governed by spiritual values, he tried to raise the sights of his listeners. The second half of Matthew's chapter five is a series of his sayings, each beginning with: 'You have heard that people were told in the past....' followed by: 'but now I tell you....'. Indeed, he saw his vision becoming a reality by the accepted human values being turned upside down:

The lowly are exalted and the mighty brought low (Luke 1:52).

The poor, the children, the lepers and the powerless, all those on the fringe of society, are those who matter (Matthew 19:13-15).

The first shall be last and the last first (Mark 10:31).

The greatest becomes the least, the servant of all (Mark 10:43-44).

Dignity lies in serving, not in being served (Luke 22:24-27)

Anxiety for self-promotion is death and the gift of self is life (Mark 8:35).

Not a new religion

Jesus was not requiring a change of religious affiliation. He had no intention of founding a new religion. (Flavius Josephus (c.37-c.100 CE) a Jewish historian and soldier born in Jerusalem, listed Christianity as one of the four major sects of Judaism, along with the Pharisees, Sadducees and Essenes.)

The challenge of Jesus was to a change of heart, a change of attitude. But it was more than a personal conversion. People living these interior values would collectively bring about a new society. This is such a fundamental call to today's creative Christian to bring about the Jesus vision for a new world, that we will devote the next chapter to this subject. What is implied by his challenge is that the centuries-old hierarchical structure would become instead a community-structured society. This was a revolution indeed. So revolutionary that nowhere in the world, despite two thousand years of Christian influence, do we yet find such a social framework existing. Although, as we shall see later, with a new consciousness breaking through in our own times, particularly with the increasing appreciation of the feminine values, cracks in the old hierarchical structure are beginning to appear in western society.

The driving force behind such a revolution in society is the belief in the divinity of every human being, appreciated, not for their value to society, but for their own worth as human beings. Jesus' Kingdom vision values people for what they are: everyone a reflection of the Divine, everyone a divine incarnation. Carl Jung expressed this as: 'The pattern of God exists in every person' and we are familiar with the Quaker saying: 'There is that of God in everyone'. This, and nothing else, gives the true value to every human being.

This was the insight which gave focus to Jesus' vision: this ability to recognise the presence of the Divine not only in every creature but in all of creation.

His creative mind could picture a new world made possible by all those he encountered having their consciousness raised to the same awareness of the divine presence and ordering their lives accordingly. Then one's enemy is no longer perceived as an enemy, a rival no longer as a rival. Jesus' world is a world of unconditional love. An impossible dream? It was lived by this one man who lived his vision. A few others, dotted through history over the last two thousand years have lived this vision too. But they are indeed few. Perhaps the urgency and depth of our present world crisis will shake us up enough to recognise that there is another way of living, another way of ordering society.

A way of life

The Jesus vision has come to be so eclipsed by the prominence of the institution which promulgates it, that one can easily forget that Jesus did not preach dogma, nor found an institution, but introduced us to a new 'Way' of living.

Jesus referred to himself as 'the Way' (John 14:6). Human beings are wanderers, always on the way. But which way? We may know our destination, but the turns we take may lead to dead ends or take us on a meandering route. The Israelites in the desert trusted that God would show them the way to a new life. 'To show you the way, He went in front of you in a pillar of fire by night and in a pillar of cloud by day' (Deuteronomy 1:33). Jesus leads those who follow him along the way to a fuller life, which is why he could say in the same sentence: 'I am the Way, the Truth and the Life' (John 14:6).

The earliest Christian community was referred to as 'The Way'.

Before his conversion, Paul persecuted 'some of the followers of that Way, men and women alike' (Acts 9:2) and confessed later: 'I persecuted till death the people who followed this Way' (22:4). There are further references in the Acts of the Apostles to this new Way. We are told of Apollos (18:24-25) that 'he was an eloquent speaker and had a thorough knowledge of the Scriptures. He had been instructed in the Way of the Lord.' However, he was not getting the message quite right so 'when Priscilla and Aquila heard him they took him home with them and explained the Way to him more correctly' (18:26). Paul went to the synagogue in Ephesus to speak to his fellow Jews 'trying to convince them about the Kingdom of God' but some would not believe and 'said evil things about the Way of the Lord' (19:8-9). Later, Paul declared: 'I worship the God of our ancestors by following that Way which they call a sect' (24:14).

A call to a higher state of consciousness

I have already said that Jesus lived in a high state of consciousness. He made it clear that this was a condition for anyone attempting to live his vision in practice. The earliest account we have of his announcing the break-through of this new world order is given by Mark: 'The right time has come and the Kingdom of God is at hand. Repent and believe this Good News' (1:15). The word 'repent' is an unfortunate translation into English of the word *metanoia* in Greek, the language in which the gospel was written. It gives us the impression that Jesus is saying 'express sorrow', 'be converted', 'feel your guilt', 'make reparation'. *Metanoia* has a much deeper meaning than that. Literally it means beyond the mind, just as *metaphysics* means beyond, greater than the physical. What Jesus is saying is 'change your mind-set, put on a new mind' or as we might say today: 'transcend your level of consciousness to understand this Good News'. Jesus expressed this in another way to the Jewish leader Nicodemus who crept to him for instruction by night. 'No one can see the Kingdom of God unless he is born again' (John 3:3). It is that much different from our everyday level of consciousness, from our rational knowledge.

We have no record in our New Testament scriptures, nor in contemporary literature, that Jesus ever imparted a higher esoteric teaching. However, reading between the lines of the gospel accounts it would seem that he did impart some secret knowledge to those closest to him. As is the way with all true spiritual masters, he imparted only that level of teaching that each was able to digest. 'He told them as much as they could understand' (Mark 4:33). To the crowds he gave basic ethical norms to enable them to live more in accord with what he understood as God's design for humanity. By his employing parables as the medium of his message each one in the crowd was able to comprehend the teaching at their own level of consciousness (Matthew 13:34). Mark writes: 'He spoke the word to them [the crowd] as far as they were capable of understanding it .... but he explained everything to his disciples when they were alone' (4:33-34). We certainly do not know everything Jesus taught. The very last words of the gospel of John are: 'There are many other things that Jesus did. If they were all written down one by one, I suppose that the whole world could not contain the books that would have to be written' (21:25).

To a chosen few Jesus said: 'The knowledge of the secrets of the Kingdom of God has been given to you, but to the rest it comes by means of parables' (Luke 8:10). We can only guess that 'the secrets of the Kingdom of God' were a ritual or a technique for entering into a higher state of consciousness – not unlike the Eastern methods of meditation we can learn today – by which the divine indwelling could be experienced. (I shall expand upon this in Chapter 11.) Where might Jesus himself have obtained such knowledge? We cannot overlook the possibility that Jesus might have learned some form of Eastern meditation during those 'hidden years' which preceded his three years of preaching. After all, Palestine was on the trade route between East and West and we notice that a number of his parables have their parallel in early Eastern literature. In his time there were already Buddhist monks living in Egypt.

If he did teach those nearest to him a higher spiritual path, – and he did say: 'I have told you everything I have heard from my Father' (John 15:15) – why was this not passed down by them? Why has such valuable instruction been lost to us? The gospels were written for the ordinary people, for their level of comprehension, so they did not include any private instructions his disciples might have received.

His appeal

Laurie Beth Jones, a business consultant in the United States, was struck by the way in which Jesus' approach to leadership differed so greatly from today's management styles. Two questions nagged at her. How could one person train a mere handful of followers in only three years, such that they went on to influence the whole world, and how did he achieve this with men who 'in spite of illiteracy, questionable backgrounds, fractious feelings and momentary cowardice, went on to accomplish the task he gave them to do'? In her book *Jesus, CEO* (Chief Executive Officer) she expands on three categories of his strengths: the strength of self-mastery, the strength of action and the strength of relationships.

Under the first she notes that everything he said about himself was positive. Nowhere in the gospels does Jesus put himself down. He was very clear about who he was and what he came to do, and never deviated from it. He did not look for approval from external agents: his actions were not based on what Peter or James or John thought of him. He conserved his energy for his mission. He refused to engage in meaningless debates with people who wanted not to learn but to argue. He never wasted energy begging or manipulating others to follow him. After his discourse to the crowds explaining how he was the Bread of Life (John 6) many turned away with incomprehension: 'This teaching is too hard'. 'Many of Jesus' followers turned back and would not go with him any more. So he asked the twelve disciples, "And you – would you also like to leave?"'(John 6:66-67). He respected their freedom.

His single-mindedness enabled him to do the difficult things. Determined to go to Jerusalem and meet the fate he expected, he did not let the pleas of Peter stop him (Matthew 16:21-23). He said no to his mother when she tried to interrupt his teaching (Mark 3:31-33).

Then there is his strength of action. He knew his mission would be fruitful because he was doing his Father's work: 'My Father is always working and I too must work.' (John 5:15). He was clear about what was of the Kingdom of God and what was not. Forty of his parables tell us what the Kingdom is like and twenty-five warn about the fate of those who are unprepared for the Kingdom. Jesus knew he could not change his Jewish people alone so he formed a team. Whom he chose is instructive. He did not invite the learned in Jewish law, the intellectuals, but people who were drawn to him by his own magnetism and excited by his vision of life. He chose heart people, not head people. He did not join the contemporary leadership: the Pharisees were dysfunctional religious leaders, enslaving people. Jesus saw his role as setting people free to develop their potential, to mature. 'I have come in order that you might have life – life in all its fullness' (John 10:10).

It is recognized today that EQ is twice as important as IQ in the workplace. For leadership posts employers look for 15% IQ and 85% EQ. For what Abraham Maslow, the psychologist, calls self-actualisation, our greatest need is for meaning, for purpose in life. Jesus gave his followers just that.

Thirdly, there is the strength of his relationships. He gave himself completely to each encounter. When the rich young man came to him 'Jesus looked straight at him with love' (Mark 10:21). He saw the inner person in each one. His single-mindedness about his mission did not cause him to thrust ahead regardless. He invited people's ideas. 'What do you want me to do for you?', he asked the blind beggar (Mark 10:51). He encouraged people to ask for things rather than dictate to them what they needed (Matthew 7:7-10). Contrary to the custom of the time, he empowered women (Matthew 28:9-10, Luke 8:2-3). He taught the importance of forgiveness and was quick to practise it himself when Peter three times denied knowing him (John 21:15-17), and supremely by his prayer while dying on the cross for those who had nailed him there: 'Forgive them, Father. They do not know what they are doing' (Luke 23:34). He kept company as much with the thieves, the prostitutes, the tax-collectors as with the wealthy merchants. He must surely have reflected joy and laughter. He attracted children. People felt good about themselves in his presence.

The good news becomes diluted

Sad to say, the Jesus vision of the world, the way it might be, has been all but lost over the last two thousand years, and overlooked by the very body, the Church, whose mission it is to proclaim Jesus' Good News. Why is this so?

One contributing factor might be this. Every Sunday millions of Christians around the world recite a 4th century Creed in their worship. Apart from the many items in this list of beliefs – which increasingly more Christians are having difficulty in voicing! – is the strange fact that it passes straight from the birth of Jesus to his death, omitting what is the very core message that he came among us to announce. There is no mention in this statement of his vision nor of his empowering us to bring it about. To understand the reason for this omission we need to recall (from Chapter 2) why the Creed was written in the first place.

Christianity grew slowly, taking many different forms. It was never one homogeneous community spreading evenly through what is now Europe. In fact the first differences of opinion of what the Jesus event was all about, occurred within decades of his death. The major division was between those apostles who were based in Jerusalem under the leadership of James 'the brother of the Lord', who insisted that Jesus had no other intention than to reform his own religion, and the disciples of Paul who, supported by a vision that Peter had experienced (Acts 10) understood that the Jesus message was for all races. After his vision Peter had to declare: 'I now realise that it is true that God treats everyone on the same basis. Whoever worships him and does what is right is acceptable to him, no matter what race he belongs to' (10:34-35). With this belief Paul and his companions went out into the Gentile lands of Asia Minor and as far as Rome, the heart of the pagan Empire.

Ideas differ with time

As local communities of Christians were formed, different ideas about the person and mission of Jesus began to be expressed. We notice this in their writings. For Peter, Jesus was a man 'raised up by God' (Acts 2:23-36). For Matthew, writing for his fellow Jews, he was the promised Messiah. So Matthew's text is peppered with references to the Hebrew Scriptures (the Christians' Old Testament) to make the point that Jesus was the fulfilment of the Messianic prophecies. The Gospels of Mark and Luke present Jesus as a miracle-worker and healer, who received the Spirit of God and through his loyalty to his mission, even to the point of dying for it, is raised up to be the Christ (or 'Messiah' in Hebrew). In the letter to the community in Ephesus the author presents Jesus as a glorious Cosmic Christ. By the time John's Gospel was written, around the turn of the century, Jesus had become the pre-existent Word of God, a quite other-worldly figure: 'The Word made flesh'. On the other hand, to the unknown author of the Letter to the Hebrews Jesus was 'tempted in every way we are, but did not sin' (4:15). Different perceptions of a founder figure give rise to differing communities of followers.

By the time Emperor Constantine became a Christian in 312 (although he was baptised only on his deathbed in 337) there were a series of Churches existing alongside each other and in many cases manifesting some rivalry. This was divisive and dangerous to Constantine's rule, as was related in the last chapter. A single like-minded Church would strengthen the Empire. To bring this about he called the bishops together for a Council at Nicaea in 325 and presided over it himself. Two hundred and twenty bishops were in attendance, from Egypt and Syria in the East and from Italy and Spain in the West. He demanded that they produce one statement of belief, acceptable to all. The result was the Nicene Creed but not quite as we have it today. Since the main controversy was between the views of Arius and those of Athanasius about the nature of the divinity of Jesus (the bishops voted 218 to 2 in favour of Athanasius) the last section of the Creed read:

> But the Holy Catholic and Apostolic Church anathematises
> those who say that there was a time when the Son of God
> was not, and that before being begotten he was not, and who
> declare that he was made from nothing; or who assert that the

Son of God is from a different substance or essence than the
Father or is subject to change or alteration.

The Council was a political victory for Constantine.

Because its statements were required only to address the points
upon which disagreement had been expressed, there is no inclusion of
the vision Jesus proclaimed. In consequence, as we have already said,
the very reason for Jesus' life ('I must preach the Good News of the
Kingdom of God .... because that is what God sent me to do' (Luke
4:43) has become lost. Little wonder that the prevalent understanding
among church-goers to this day as to the reason for Jesus' mission, is
that he was sent by his Father to shed his blood and die as a sacrifice
for our salvation. His death and resurrection is perceived as the
redeeming event, the purpose of his life. His central message has been
obscured, lost sight of.

If Jesus' creativity is to be of benefit to us in the 21st century we
have to come to a contemporary understanding of his vision and
express it in a language and in imagery which relate to our present-
day culture and values. All expressions of truth are relative to the time
and culture and circumstance which provoke them. (Similarly, what is
considered an expression of heresy is also relative to time and culture
and the current theological understanding!) We have to liberate
ourselves from what we were taught as children in Sunday School or
Catechism class, to look anew, as mature adults, at the creative mind
of Jesus expressed by the metaphor 'The Kingdom of God'. We might
take our cue from the author of the Letter to the Hebrews: 'Let us go
forward, then, to mature teaching and leave behind us the first lessons
[we received] of the Christian message' (6:1).

4 The Jesus shape of society

WHEREVER we human beings live together we form a social structure to regulate our relationships. This ranges from the family unit – whether nuclear or extended – to the village, town, state or nation. Each is a search for an ideal way to share life and promote our mutual dependence in peace and friendship. But because of our inability as ego-centred creatures to share life fully, openly – because we dare not take the risk of that – our relationships are strained by fear. We overcome our fear by dominating that which we fear. So our social structures, instead of being life-enhancing for everyone, become structures of oppression for the many. Instead of giving a fuller life to others, we – mostly subconsciously – take life and freedom from others 'to keep them in their place'. We have only to look at our daily newspapers to be reminded of how domination gives birth to violence, whether it be the collective violence of a suppressed racial minority or the violence of frustrated individuals deprived of security, of a job prospect, of an opening to improve themselves. Our world economic system causes the few to dominate the many. Today we are seeing this on a global scale. Ten percent of the human population is classified as affluent, consuming more than three-quarters of the planet's resources, and will go to any lengths to keep it that way. The perpetuation of domination in our human society, since it is a power structure, is due to our failure to be fully human: our failure to love unconditionally.

It is difficult for us today to imagine how society can be ordered in any other than in a hierarchical shape. But, as we will see later, Jesus had a vision of another way of ordering society.

The origins of hierarchy

As far back as we can trace in our western religious history – to Abraham's time, some 4,000 years ago – we already see society based on a pyramid or hierarchy model. But there is evidence that further back still it was not so. The hierarchy model, which is a male-dominated model, seems to have become the pattern when our ancestors took the evolutionary step from being hunter-gatherers to developing skills in agriculture and animal husbandry. The development of agriculture required more stable communities needing to possess land they could call their own and defend against invaders. Defence meant the need to fight. The need to fight , required male warriors. The tribes that developed cattle breeding required more and more grazing land so, unlike the settled farmers, they became nomads. They too had their male warriors to conquer the pastures their cattle needed.

Between 4,300 and 2,800 BCE three major waves of nomadic cattle herders of Indo-European or Aryan-language-speaking stock swept down into Europe from the Asiatic and European north-east. Led by powerful priests and warriors they brought into Europe their male gods of war. What kind of society did they encounter, and gradually overturn? In her fascinating book *The Chalice and the Blade* Riane Eisler reports from her research that in the Neolithic period (10,000 – 4,000 BCE) our ancestors worshipped the creator as a goddess, one who gave fertility, and not as a male god. Consequently the feminine values of creativity and nurturing were uppermost over the male values of domination and rule by fear or threat. Eisler presents plenty of evidence that during this period people lived in a non-male-dominated, non-hierarchical society. Although it was a matrilineal society, in which descent and inheritance were traced through the mother, it was not a female-dominated society. It was an egalitarian society in which women played key roles in all aspects of life. From the absence of any signs of heavy fortifications or throwing weapons belonging to this period we can deduce that it was a peace-loving society.

The Semitic people who invaded Canaan from the South were also nomadic herdsmen ruled by warriors and priests, the Levites, and brought with them a male god of war: Yahweh. Chapter 21 of the Book of Numbers describes Yahweh's instructions to Moses for a war of revenge against the Midianites. Yahweh gave clear instructions about the distribution of booty between the soldiers, the priests and the community (in that order of importance). Eisler writes: 'The one thing they [the invaders] all had in common was a dominator model of social organisation: a social system in which male dominance, male violence and a generally hierarchic and authoritarian social structure was the norm'. This is the shape society had in Jesus' day. A higher value was put on the power that takes life than on the power that gives life.

Of divine origin?

It is sometimes argued that we were created to be hierarchy creatures; that the structure is born from the struggle for the power which we feel is necessary to survive in society. The argument is based upon observations made of the animal kingdom. Take, for example, the chimpanzee, a native of Central Africa. Chimpanzees are one of the four great apes (with gorillas, orang-utans and gibbons) but closer to us than the others. The ape family split off from our own branch of the evolutionary tree. We can call them our 'cousins' since we have 98.5% of our DNA in common. (What a difference 1.5% can make!) We observe that chimpanzees have their own pecking order which is respected when it comes to rivalry for the leadership of their extended family. So is the hierarchy pattern in our genes?

Others argue that the hierarchy paradigm is of divine origin because the source of all power is God and God is 'above' creation. But then we have to ask, what is the origin of that belief? Which came first, the notion that God is 'above' and outside creation and that therefore perfection and power must be at the pyramid's peak, or did the human creation of the hierarchy structure cause humanity to conclude that God must be 'at the top'?

We have to remember that the creation accounts of Jewish mythology were written only a few hundred years before the Jesus event, by which time the Chosen People had already experienced being structured into a hierarchical society with a king at the top, a king of divine choice. By that time they were city-dwellers, male-dominated, belligerent – (we read in I Chronicles 20:1, 'In the Spring, at the time of the year when kings usually go to war ...') – the men had gained ascendancy over women and the rational mind had come to dominate the intuitive. It does not surprise us then to read in the very first chapter of Genesis of an external God, powerful, who creates 'man' and then creates a woman out of a part of man, a woman who is reported to be the one tempted by an evil serpent and responsible for 'the Fall'. It shows how much female creative power had become debased. We read of God saying: 'Now we will make human beings; they will be like us and resemble us. They will have *power* over the fish, the birds and all animals, domestic and wild, large and small' and later on instructing Adam and Eve to 'fill the Earth and *conquer* it'. This was a human projection onto God as creator, of the social structure that was already in place. Sadly, it is upon this biblical base that we of the Western religions, acknowledging Abraham as our common father, have given ourselves authority to dominate all the rest of creation at our whim; to use it for our benefit, to destroy it even. We still speak of 'the conquest of nature'. Incidentally, having dominion over the animals (Genesis 1:26) did not include killing them for food (1:29). That permission is given only later (9:3) to Noah.

Hierarchy is about power

The hierarchical paradigm is not of divine origin but is a human construct upon which divine authority has been bestowed. Once a power structure pertains – and hierarchy is all about the possession and use of power – a power grading takes place. Absolute power is at the pinnacle and trickles downwards, the powerless being 'at the bottom of the stack'. It demands obedience to the level above and assumes domination over the level below. It is a structure of control. It breeds fear, fear of failure, and is therefore the enemy of risking anything new.

In the Judeo-Christian tradition (and in most other cultures) men are above women while children are beneath adults, with adults owning and controlling children; the fit are held to be of more value than the disabled. The worth of each is measured by their value to society, which in turn is measured by their achievement. How many women still describe their role in life as 'I'm only a housewife'? The role of women in the home has no value by the achievement measurement.

Hierarchy is the tool used to conserve order. Two obvious examples of this are the army and the Church, in both of which control is considered to be essential.

In its very earliest days the young Church was not hierarchical. Paul addresses his letters, not to the leaders, but to the community, 'the brothers'. As the number of Christians grew their structure began to model itself on the Roman Empire. The later 'Pastoral' letters (to Timothy and Titus) reveal a hierarchy model beginning to emerge. The very word 'hier-archy' was coined by Dionysius, a 6th century monk in Syria, to denote the totality of ruling persons in the Church. Hier-archy means sacred government and we speak of those with power in ecclesiastical society, the Bishops, as 'The Hierarchy', from whom instructions, doctrines and precepts filter down.

The Jesus model

But Jesus proposed a different model. His ideal for humanity was radical. He was able to envisage how it could be otherwise. Sadly though, only a few years after Pentecost, Jesus' small group of followers were so unable to situate themselves in another social shape than that around them that they began to organise their converts on the pattern of the contemporary civil state and themselves to assume the role in the new community that the Pharisees and Sadducees were playing in the Jewish nation.

But this is not how it is to be in the Kingdom of God. Jesus cut right through the traditions of his society and in doing so challenged people – and us – to see that there is another way of ordering our relationships.

Nowhere in the Gospels do we find Jesus approving the hierarchy model of society. Quite the contrary, as we see in the instruction he gave to those who were to be leaders in his new community:

> You know that the men who are considered to be rulers of the heathen have power over them, and the leaders have complete authority. This, however, is not the way it is among you. If one of you wants to be great, he must be the servant of the rest; and if one of you wants to be first, he must be the slave of all. For even the Son of Man did not come to be served; he came to serve (Mark 10:42-45).

This was said to them after they had been prospecting for positions in the Kingdom of glory.

Hierarchy values us for what we *have* or for what we can contribute from what we have: our role, our abilities, our leadership skills, our honours and titles, our education, our class or caste. In such a paradigm we are what we are, only by being measured against others. Our worth, even in our own eyes – our self-worth – depends upon how others regard us. This breeds the ethos of competition. By contrast the community paradigm (as I shall call that demanded by the Kingdom vision) values us for what we *are*. It is non-competitive. Our worth comes from our being of value to and beloved by God, because there is that of God in us. In Jesus' perspective we are acceptable because we are a brother or sister of the same Father.

The parable of the wedding feast (Matthew 22:2-10) in which the king's servants are sent out into the streets to invite just anyone in to sit at the same table – female and male, married and unmarried, slave and free, pure and impure, rich and poor – reveals Jesus' radical egalitarianism in which discrimination and social position no longer have a place.

When mothers brought children to Jesus, his companions scolded them, as much as to say: 'Jesus has more important people to bless and heal than mere children'. But we are told that Jesus was angry with his disciples and what he said about the Kingdom of God being as much for children as for adults reveals again that he did not judge a person's worth by their place in society (Mark 10:13-16). He had no time for the pomp of the 'teachers of the law and the Pharisees' (Matt.23:6-10).

In a parable, Jesus has the master turn servant: 'How happy are those servants whose master finds them awake and ready when he returns. I tell you, he will take off his cloak, ask them to sit down and will wait on them' (Luke 12:37).

Later, Jesus was to turn his words into action to illustrate the form he expected leadership to take in the Kingdom community. While at supper with his disciples 'he rose from the table, took off his outer garment and tied a towel around his waist. Then he poured some water into a basin and began to wash the disciples' feet and dry them with the towel round his waist'. He concluded his lesson by saying: 'I, your Lord and Master, have just washed your feet. You then should wash one another's feet. I have set an example for you, so that you will do just what I have done for you' (John 13:4-15).

It was on another occasion at table that 'Jesus noticed how some of the guests were choosing the best places, so he told this parable to all of them: "When someone invites you to a wedding feast, do not sit down in the best place. It could happen that someone more important than you has been invited ... instead, when you are invited go and sit in the lowest place ... for everyone who makes himself great will be humbled, and everyone who humbles himself will be made great"'(Luke 14:7-11).

Contrary to the prevailing custom Jesus did not treat women as being in any way inferior to men. He had special concern for the marginalised, the outcasts, for lepers, for the public sinners, for the despised tax-collectors. Roles played no part in the way he valued people. The Pharisees recognised this. When sent to challenge Jesus they began with: 'We know that you tell the truth, without worrying about what people think. A man's rank means nothing to you...' (Mark 12:14).

In the hierarchy paradigm we give greater credence when a person is thought 'to speak with authority', because of their position in society's pecking order. Jesus was often asked by what authority he said the outrageous things people heard. But he never replied directly to that question. The authenticity of what he said – people just knew at their deepest level that what he said was right – gave it its own authority. It matched their experience: it 'rang true'.

If the very essence of living by Kingdom values is to be conscious of the divine dimension in oneself, in other people and in all of nature, – as Karl Jung put it: 'the pattern of God exists in every man' – then acting upon that appreciation will govern all our relationships.

Jesus' vision is breaking through

Now, two thousand years on, we can see encouraging signs that humanity is taking small steps to move from a hierarchy society to a community society. Let us look at five contemporary signs which, I suggest, reveal that a paradigm shift is beginning to come about which favours the Kingdom of God becoming a reality.

Authority is being questioned

The hierarchy structure is a structure of command: the domination of some requiring the obedience of others. Obedience to authority was drummed into us from our earliest years. Today, for a whole variety of reasons, the authority of those 'in authority' is being questioned. Just because a person is a teacher or a parent or a priest or a politician it does not follow that we owe them blind obedience. A more highly educated population asks questions, wants to make its own responsible decisions, needs to challenge the assumptions of 'leaders'. Young people are no longer willing to give docile obedience to father-figures unless such a person's authority is felt to be authentic, by which they mean that it is authenticated by their own experience. People world-wide are no longer happy to have others decide their future or their children's future, but want to have a say in it themselves. Witness the universal move towards democracy.

Equal opportunities

Secondly, there is currently a reaction against male domination and a desire for women and men to have equal opportunities. This is as true among the laity in the Church as it is in the professions. Traditional roles are even being reversed, often for economic reasons: the man becomes the house-husband while the woman is the bread-winner. In society at large, men are no longer automatically awarded a position above women. But there is something deeper at play than the liberalis-ing of women. It is the appreciation of what we have come to call the feminine values – intuition, creativity, compassion, nurturing – and the desire that they, along with the masculine values, need to be in bal-ance in every human being, irrespective of gender.

A progression towards human rights

Thirdly, there is growing concern throughout the world for 'human rights'. Respect for the individual's worth is a preliminary step towards forming a communitarian society in which everyone's intrinsic worth is valued. We are familiar with the declaration of human rights that was made during the French Revolution of the late 18th century calling for 'Liberty, Equality, Fraternity'. The very idea, which we regard as quite normal today, struck fear into the political and ecclesiastical leaders at the time. Pope Pius VI (1775-1799) strongly condemned this manifesto of the Revolution.

We witness the progression of waves towards personal freedom if we list the series of emancipations in our recent history: absolute monarchy being replaced by democracy, emancipation from slavery, the emancipation of women from male domination (claiming the right to possess property, to have a vote, to enjoy social equality and to have equal career opportunities). The emancipation of children from child labour, – the boy chimney sweeps – at least in the West. The emancipation of colonies from foreign imperialism, of coloured races from white supremacy, and more recently of homosexuals from heterosexual righteousness. Each emancipation has been a struggle against the fierce resistance of those wishing to maintain the contemporary pattern of society.

This concern throughout the world for 'human rights' is the acknowledgement of the innate value of every human being. Within recent decades we have had the publication of a Universal Declaration of Human Rights (1948) and indeed the creation of a body able to draw up and have the authority to publish such a document: the United Nations, witnessing our world-wide inter-dependence. Some have regarded this document as the expression of God's Will for our own time, spelling out as it does, the deepest aspirations of the human heart for the well-being of all humanity.

There is a long list of Non-Governmental Organisations (NGOs) and Aid Agencies concerned with justice issues, not forgetting the innumerable smaller groups giving voice to the struggle of particular ethnic minorities. Such concerns as the elimination of Third World Debt stir hundreds of thousands of us into action with the conviction that each one of us can make a difference, each has a contribution to make towards bettering this world.

But the demand for the rights of every individual is only the first step towards the community structure. Now we need a Universal Declaration of Human Duties! When everyone has a sense of their duty to others, the rights of each will automatically be respected. Rights breed individualism: duties breed community.

Change originates at the grass roots

Fourthly, the initiative for change for better is no longer expected to filter down from on high. Change is born at the grassroots and what is giving power to this source of change today is 'networking'. The power to forge our future lies in the large number of ordinary people with their creativity and enthusiasm pooling their ideas and resources by networking. This is 'people power'. This is given a reinforcement, a new ability, in our own time with the rapid spread of the 'World Wide Web'. The Internet is a tremendous equaliser. It ignores time and distance. Anyone, anywhere, with no need to advertise their 'authority' can post their point of view on everyone else's screen. There is no controlling parent figure to censor or disapprove. By networking, power is exercised horizontally. This is the new force shaping world opinion and bringing about change.

Globalisation

Globalisation accounts for another crack in the hierarchy paradigm. The word was first used in the context of a global economy but it now encompasses the great new phenomenon of our time, the integration of all aspects of life into one world-wide network. So we need to distinguish between globalisation in its broadest sense, the world become a global village, and corporate globalisation. Whereas the latter is a trade and finance based strategy by which transnational companies strive for world-wide economic power through such bodies as the World Trade Organisation, the former embodies a spiritual dimension. It is with this latter that we are concerned here because it can be understood as a movement towards the fulfilment of that unity of all humanity for which Jesus prayed.

Despite all the negative issues that are laid at globalisation's door, like the eclipse of particular cultures by a new global culture, it does mark the end of the supremacy of the Christian West. Although numerically there are more Christians in the southern hemisphere today than in the northern, culturally Christianity has always been western and western culture over the last two millennia has been Christian. The certainties that underpinned western society, that gave it the moral right to attempt to colonise the rest of the world, derived from belief in the unchangeable values of the Bible. But cultural

Christianity is at an end.

The ideal is for all of humanity to order its life together by Kingdom values, ordered by interior, spiritual power rather than by external human-controlled power. No Kingdom values are so particular, so unique, that they are not found in all religions. Kingdom values are human values when a person is living by the highest values of humanity, to our full potential, living the life we were created to live.

5 The challenge of Jesus' vision – then and now

I N Chapter 3 we saw that the energising spirit that activated Jesus' vision was his ability to recognise the existence of the Divine in every human being and in all creation. He felt one with all creation: 'My Father has given me all things' (Luke 10:22), 'All that my Father has is mine' (John 16:15). As a consequence of which he appreciated the inter-relationship of everyone because each person contains that same spark of the Divine, though manifested more clearly in some than in others, the same divinity which was so clearly manifest in his own life.

It was this insight that drove him to challenge the *status quo*. Bearing in mind his being a product of and living immersed in Jewish culture, it could be nothing less than the power of his mystical experience that led him to challenge it head on. The ethos of Jewish culture, as we have just seen, was hierarchical and patriarchal. Positions in society were its foundation. Being a religious society, the position of people was based on their purity rating. Holiness was equated with purity. The categories of 'pure' and 'impure' were applied to both individuals and social groups. On this scale, priests and Levites came top, followed by true Israelites: all who were Jewish by birth. Then came 'converts', Jews who were not Jewish by birth. At the bottom were those who were regarded as bastards. Physical wholeness and wealth (a sign of God's blessing) were considered indications of purity, while at the other end of the social scale were such impure people as the 'outcasts', among whom were tax-collectors, prostitutes, but also dice players, usurers, bath masters, tanners, camel drivers, butchers and even shepherds.

Men were held to be more pure than women, hence women could not be witnesses, and had few of the rights of men. Women, like children, were nobodies. Needless to say, Gentiles were impure and unclean, beyond the pale. So degrees of purity or impurity determined the whole social order. Consequently a lot of the customs and rites were about preserving purity. (In the parable of the Good Samaritan the priest and the Levite would not approach the half-dead victim because contact with the dead was a major impurity.)

Jesus, recognizing the divinity of every human being, shocked the Jewish establishment because of his complete disregard for this scale of values. So dramatic was the attitudinal change he proposed that it became confrontational. He had an alternative social vision. It was of a community based on compassion. 'Be compassionate just as your Father is compassionate' (Luke 6:36). He lived what he preached. He touched lepers and haemorrhaging women, he entered a graveyard to cure a man who lived among (impure) pigs. He shared meals with the impure, was accused of eating with tax collectors and sinners: 'The Pharisees and the teachers of the Law started grumbling: "This man welcomes outcasts and even eats with them"' (Luke 15:2). His was to be a world of non-discrimination. He spoke with Gentile women. Paul and the early Christians furthered the message: 'In Christ there is neither Jew nor Gentile, slave nor free, male nor female' (Galatians 3:28) and in his letter to the Colossians Paul wrote: 'There is no longer any distinction between Gentiles and Jews, circumcised and uncircumcised, barbarians, savages, slaves and free men, but Christ is all, Christ is in all' (3:11).

Sadly, as the Good News of Jesus spread further into Asia Minor and on to Rome, the model of the Roman social structure took over and the organisation of the early Church assumed a hierarchical structure. In both the Church and in western society that structure is with us still, but with this difference: it is based not on religious purity but controlled by power and wealth.

The two great and complementary thrusts of Jesus' proclamation were for personal transformation – being born again by the Spirit into a 'new creation' (John 3:5) – and the means was to follow 'The Way' (as we said in Chapter 3), while the second was the transformation of society, described in terms of the 'Kingdom of God'. This latter was a political statement, but unfortunately, with Christianity becoming the state religion under the Emperor Constantine (4th C), the Kingdom message became understood as referring to personal salvation – a means of reaching the Kingdom of Heaven – and the radical idea of a this-world society of justice and mercy were interpreted to mean personal ethical behaviour. And so it has been understood to this day. Marcus Borg writes: 'The Way is spiritual, the Kingdom is political'.

Contemporary motivations

Although it is to only a minority today that the example of Jesus speaks, his vision, nevertheless, can be recognised as dawning upon our world for other than religious reasons. We see emerging a new way of thinking about our social structures and for discounting our national, ethnical, cultural, linguistic differences, in order to build up the human community. We are becoming more aware that to do so is our only hope of surviving as the human race on planet Earth.

In yet another perspective, we can appreciate our fundamental relationship as issuing from our common origin, from the fact that we – and not only persons but everything on Earth and the planets and galaxies too – are all the product of the Big Bang. As is frequently said, we are all formed from stardust, the remnants of that super-nova which brought forth our Universe.

Scientists approach the foundation of our relationships from yet an-other angle. They speak of our inter-relatedness and of our consequential interdependence, in terms of the theory of Quantum Physics.

Our mutual interdependence

A human being does not live in isolation but in association. This is so obvious at the physical level. We have simply to think of all the people involved in providing us with our breakfast. Not only the growers and processors and traders of what we ate, but the makers of the plates and cutlery and the chair and table, the hundreds involved in providing the electricity and what generated it, enabling us to boil a kettle, indeed the builders of the very house in which we have eaten breakfast.

At the mind (I.Q.) and at the emotional (E.Q.) levels, we are what we are in great measure due to the millions of influences, beginning with our parents, which have touched our lives from conception till this moment. We may even feel that our identity depends upon other peoples' regard for us. Anne Bancroft speaks of this in *The Luminous Vision*:

> When we derive our identity only from our interaction with other people, we then need others to accept and reaffirm our existence and we often spend considerable time and energy striving for this recognition. Our derived identity, made up of all our many appearances, becomes our most precious possession – without it we think we would cease to be.

How true the famous expression of John Donne: 'No man is an island, entire of itself'. In a book of that title the Cistercian monk and mystic Thomas Merton wrote: 'Every other man is a piece of myself, for I am a part and a member of mankind. ... What I do is also done for them and with them and by them. What they do is in me and by me and for me'.

Our religious interdependence

Equally at the religious level, my beliefs and my interpretation of spiritual experiences are arrived at from what I have received from others. In my own case, from a Christian source. The reason I am a Christian today and not a Muslim or Buddhist is because I was brought up in the context of my parents' beliefs which were those of our national heritage. As an adult I have chosen freely to continue with the Christian belief system because with my background it is that which to my mind most adequately and most satisfactorily, though relatively, answers the most fundamental questions about life. Within this framework, however, I am continually re-adjusting my understanding of the truths of this religion. I wonder how many Christians are given the opportunity or feel the freedom to question their beliefs and make this continual re-adjustment.

There would appear to be a widening knowledge gap between what biblical scholars are saying today and the belief of the Christian in the pew. The cause is a block in communication between the two and responsible for this is surely the pastor. Even if pastors are abreast of what scholars are saying – and one must ask how up-to-date in biblical scholarship the majority of pastors are – it is a brave preacher who will risk upsetting the 'simple faith' of his flock. His remit is to nourish their spirituality, not to undermine it. But is he being honest, indeed faithful to his mission, if he continues to preach what the Church has been teaching for centuries when he knows that there is now evidence that the tradition no longer matches the facts?

To take an example: who would dare to undermine their congregation's belief in the Christmas story? Who would be so bold as to explain from the pulpit that Jesus was probably born in Nazareth (he was commonly known as 'Jesus of Nazareth') and that the Bethlehem scene with shepherds and angelic choirs and wise men from the East was not part of the belief of the first Christians? Of all the New Testament writers, Jesus' birth is mentioned only by Luke and Matthew, not so much as historical accounts but as symbolic narratives, as an embellishment to show how earlier prophecies were fulfilled in Jesus (Matthew) and that Jesus was the champion of the poor and despised (Luke).

Although there never is, of course, agreement on all points among biblical scholars, in recent decades many are discovering much more about the life and times of Jesus of Nazareth than was previously known. (I distinguish, as scholars have for some time, between the Jesus of history and the Christ of faith. Our concern here is with the former, not with the theological understanding of the Christ which is based on the letters of Paul and John's gospel and which the Church elaborated upon in later times.*)

---

* See my monograph, *'The Christ'*, for an elaboration of this distinction.

Our new insights give us an understanding of the message, the Good News, of Jesus different from the faith understanding or moralistic understanding that we mentioned in Chapter 2. His was a message of transformation: his hearers were called to become new people by relating to God, to creation, to each other in a new way.

We are persons in relationship

Our relatedness is much deeper than the useful or needful. We human beings have been truly described as 'persons in relationship' and our deepest common relationship is with the Divine at the centre of our being.

If we are to make the creative vision of Jesus a reality in our present-day world and be challenged thereby, it must be on the same basis that it was a reality for him: recognising our inter-relationship and interdependence because of our sharing the same divine life. So closely did Jesus identify his own consciousness with that of his Father that he described it as being as necessary to his life as food: 'My food is to obey the will of the one who sent me' (John 4:34). He understood that the Divine Will was to bring about harmony in all creation.

Our personal creativity (C.Q.) is brought into play when we relate the creative vision of Jesus to our own lives and to our present world situation in an evolving Universe.

We go on in the next chapters to consider the meaning and implications of an evolving attitudinal relationship at four levels:

An evolving relationship with ourselves
  which will contribute towards
    an evolving relationship between human beings and between nations
      which will make for
        an evolving relationship between humanity and our planet
          all of which are related to
            an evolving relationship with the Transcendent.

PART TWO

Living as a Creative Christian

"It was not for any fault on the part of creation that it was made unable to attain its purpose, it was made so by God.

From the beginning till now the entire creation, as we know it, has been groaning in one great act of giving birth."
Romans 8:20,22

6 An evolving relationship with oneself

O UR ability to be creative, to expand our imagination, is particularly influenced by our attitude because our attitude determines the orientation of our life at the deepest level.

I have a long-standing friend now in her 'third age' who would be described as 'a devout Catholic'. Family upbringing in Ireland, convent school education. For whatever reason, her attitude to life I can only describe as negative. She sees evil everywhere. Her world is torn apart by, on the one side 'the Good God' bestowing his blessings and, on the other, Satan – for her a real supernatural being – inducing everyone to evil. She takes the Bible literally and the Bible speaks of a devil, so there is a devil, Satan. There is no way I can call her a joy-filled person.

She cannot understand my positive attitude. Why am I so full of joy in life which enables me to see goodness and beauty everywhere and in everything? She cannot accept my saying evil is a human creation, that there is nothing and nobody 'out there' conning people into evil. Nor can she accept that evil has no existence in its own right but is the flip-side of positive energy (all energy is positive) which is misused, misdirected, used to excess. We each have such a different attitude to life, such opposite orientations to our lives. (She thinks I am a lost soul!)

Attitude

The Collins English Dictionary defines 'attitude' as:

> The way a person views something
> or tends to behave towards it,
> often in an evaluative way.

That needs unpacking. We all have our own predispositions to react in a certain way as a response to particular people or situations. For instance, if a person is said to have a hostile attitude to Mr Bloggs, she can be presumed to show evidence of disfavour or even hostility towards him and reveal an inclination to interpret negatively anything she reads or hears about him.

But how does this predisposition come about? What determines our attitudes? Since we are complex beings, there are many factors involved. Perhaps the most forceful factor is our culture. We take on board from an unquestioning early age the attitude of those among whom we are brought up, especially those of our parents. Until they are challenged, our attitudes are possessed unnoticed, just taken for granted. When challenged they might even be denied. Our culture, our parents and family, our formal education, our social standing, our religious upbringing, society's trends, maybe even our genes, all work together to establish our attitude to life and its situations. Not one of us lives a single day without our attitudes affecting our judgement.

In these times, the media is an element particularly forceful in influencing or confirming our attitudes. We might be very persuaded by the editorial policy of a particular daily paper and its manner of reflecting on events. But then we will probably have chosen to read that paper because it matches our existing attitudes! Our attitudes affect our behaviour, but equally our behaviour enforces our attitudes. If we are challenged by values contrary to our own, we will quickly find reasons for not accepting them. For instance, we might say their source is less trustworthy. So, do our attitudes not change?

Their foundation is laid at an early age by our family's values. By adulthood most of our attitudes are well integrated and highly resistant to change. They are greatly affected by our personal characteristics such as dominance, rigidity, dependency, tolerance of ambiguity. Greater intelligence and a higher education usually allow more liberal attitudes.

A politician who espouses his party's line which is inconsistent with his privately held attitude will, over time, find his attitude is being brought into line with his public persona.

The attitudes we allow to determine our outlook on life dictate the joy or misery, the pettiness or broadmindedness which govern our lives.

There are times when we find this or that attitude challenged from without. This may give a nudge to our total attitude to life like a small tugboat affecting the steady direction of a great ocean liner. Or some incident or word of another may cause us to turn inwards and examine our own attitude. None of us can exist without a whole sheaf of attitudes which together produce our overall attitude to life.

The question is, are we so set in our attitudes that we can see life in no other way? Do we want to change our attitude to life? Maybe we should be thinking in terms of healing our attitude because it is stifling our growth towards becoming a free, mature person.

We choose our attitudes

The first thing to acknowledge is that we choose our attitudes: they do not choose us. We will have imbibed them as children but as adults we hold onto them freely. No one can deprive us of spiritual freedom. Some, like Viktor Frankl and Dostoyevsky, have to learn the lesson of spiritual freedom by their being denied physical freedom in a concentration camp or in a prison. They discovered their right to choose their attitude when all other choices were denied them.

Life is a process, a schoolroom in which we learn and grow. But, as in our childhood school situation, we can choose to be a keen student or take an attitude of disinterest. Every experience, every encounter, is a learning opportunity if we are aware of it.

If we listen to our inner voice, our Higher Self, the Divine within us for the power which we can permit to over-rule our petty ego, the healing of negative attitudes can happen. However, we foster obstacles in our minds which interfere with this process. They take the form of guilt, fear, anger, resentment, low self-esteem, competition, condemnation, denial, rejection and any other judgement of ourselves or others.

Many people who received their Christian education in Sunday School or catechism class had instilled into them unconsciously emotions of guilt and fear. Of all our emotions, these are perhaps the two which most require addressing if we are to gain a more joyful, positive attitude to life. At root, they relate to our attitude to God.

Our negative emotions, such as self-doubt, jealousy, confusion, anger, resentment, condemnation can be understood as expressions of fear. Fear creeps into our relations with people who are culturally different. It is our instinctive tendency to dislike the unlike.

We must distinguish between physical fear and psychological fear. The former is a protective safeguard. It would, for instance, protect me from attempting a bungee-jump or free-fall parachuting in my advanced years! Here we are concerned with psychological or moral fear. Our creativity is diminished by fear: fear of letting go the known and tried, fear of criticism, of being ostracized, of being the odd-one-out. Creativity is nourished by appreciating what is new and different, by being open to other ways of doing, by reconciling different ideas to give birth to a brand new idea, by envisaging possibilities.

Fear stems from the belief that we are separate from our divine source or, to express it another way, that we are unaware of the degree to which we are participants in Divine Life (what John's gospel has Jesus call 'Eternal Life') and consequently we are failing to draw on our positive, divine energies.

Feeling separate from God, we can feel separate from humanity. When we cause or express this separation, we feel guilt and guilt heralds punishment. Expectation of punishment causes us to develop defences to ward off what we fear. So we are caught in a vicious circle. Our fears prevent us from experiencing life fully. The healing process lies in the letting go of fear. When there is no more fear, there is no more struggle or panic.

Five stages to healing attitudes

In her book *To See Differently*, Dr Susan Trout proposes five major stages in the process of healing attitudes. The first is to question or identify our attitude. This may happen after an event which shakes us deeply, a shattering crisis which causes us to question the very meaning and purpose of our life. This brings about the second stage: the realisation that there must be another outlook and so to explore the unknown. This stage can be accompanied by a great fear of losing everything we have held dear. We are challenged to suspend what we think is true in order to explore another way of looking at our lives.

The third stage is to make a commitment to heal our attitudes. Once made, empowerment follows. This is the means to assume full responsibility for our healing process. The fourth stage allows the process to unfold. It will be accompanied by emotional ups and downs along the way and can have no time-scale. We are all so complex and start from different places. It is not a linear process: more like a spiral in the depth of our psyche.

The final stage is to acknowledge the healing and consequent growth. Each step we take, when we notice we have become more positive, more whole, should be deliberately acknowledged. This way it becomes anchored in our innermost selves.

There is a close link between our attitude to life and our physical health. Dis-ease occurs when we are not living life in accordance with our inner truth: we are split persons. Often illness is a form of protest against a need for change. No one but ourselves can help us over this hurdle. Nobody can cure another person, be it doctor or therapist or counsellor. They can only provide the means, release the healing energies, set us on a path. All healing, physical or psychological has to come from within because negative attitudes such as jealousy, anxiety, resentment, hostility and self-pity cause stress and stress is the most common cause of dis-ease. The stress we experience is internally generated by our attitude.

It is hard to believe, but one does come across people who prefer to hold on to their illness, however unpleasant and life-limiting, than allow themselves a change of attitude. We are not our illness: we are how we handle our illness. We are not what is happening around us: we are the attitude adopted to what is happening around us.

My attitude creates my present Me, the person I experience myself to be, the person I project to others.

Life happens in the present moment

One of the means we can use in order to adjust our attitude so as to become a more whole person, is to live the present moment to the full. This is a path to the Divine proposed by the great religions of both East and West. The NOW moment is the only reality. There is no such thing as the past. There are events which preceded the present moment – we have plenty of evidence of that all around us, not to mention our history books – and they influence this present moment, but they owe their reality to our giving them a place in our thoughts right now. Similarly, there is no such thing as the future. We expect certain events are going to happen, we presume on the gift of daylight tomorrow, but the expectation is in the present moment. We imagine ourselves living at some point on a continuum between the past and the future as if we were on a conveyor belt ever moving forward. There is no such movement from past to future. There only exists the present moment.

While I was living in Zambia I went to an introductory talk advertising a Dale Carnegie self-improvement course. I have always remembered the presenter speaking of the amount of energy we all expend worrying about coming events which in nine cases out of ten either never happen or turn out quite differently. So, live the present moment fully. There is no other!

Following this practice – what Buddhists call doing everything mindfully, giving each moment's action our full attention – we are enabled to part company slowly with those negative influences which have shaped our past and our present attitude. Shed them. Unload them. They have no value in this present moment.

Besides, the present moment is the NOW moment of God, the eternal moment. Being the only reality, it touches the God reality. God has no past, no future. God just is. This is why Jesus referred to participation in Divine Life as Eternal Life, which is different from everlasting life: life continuing in a time dimension.

All conscious creatures, in the animal and plant kingdoms, live in the NOW. Only self-aware humans have a sense of past and future, a sense of time. It is we who invented time. The more technically developed we have become, the more we have enslaved ourselves to time. All our imaginings, our day dreams, our worries are either about the past (memories) or about the future (anticipations).

If there is truth in Arnold Toynbee's saying: 'History repeats itself', it is because we live with our minds in the past. If we are to have the courage to break out of a cycle of repetitions, to do something new, to become a new self, then we must release the past. Only the present matters. The present is the creative moment: the moment to become the new person we were created to be.

The fear of not being

Living the present moment more fully enables us to cope with a future that is the foundation of all fear, the ultimate fear, the fear of not-being: the fear of death.

Death is a subject about which we rarely hear a sermon – unless we are attending a funeral. It is just about the most unpopular subject of all. It has been said with some truth that in Victorian times people spoke openly about death – they were accustomed to being at the bedside of relatives dying at home – but no one spoke about sex. Today death is the unmentionable subject, while everyone speaks about sex!

Death is an unpopular topic because it brings to the surface of our minds our own fear of dying. Ernest Becker, in his Pulitzer prize-wining book *The Denial of Death*, wrote: 'The idea of death, the fear of it, haunts the human mind like nothing else'. We are motivated by two primary instincts: the survival instinct and the growth instinct. Death threatens both.

Our fear lies in the unknown. Nobody, but nobody, knows what happens to us after we die because no one has ever come back to tell us. (I can hear the Christian saying: 'Oh, but Jesus has!' In whatever manner we may understand the meaning of the Resurrection, we have to read the gospels as giving us a faith account, not a scientific account. The evangelists report that Jesus was visible only to some people and not to others. He never revealed anything about the post-Resurrection state he was in. What we would like to know is what happened to Jesus after the event we call the Ascension.) All accounts of life after death are pure speculation. They belong in the realm of faith or fantasy.

The only certainty in life is the occurrence of change. Death is our ultimate change, a transformation. It is our last and most creative act on the world stage.

From the moment we can be called a living human being, in the womb, we are destined to die. Life and death are inseparable. Everyone is young enough to die.

I have said that our ultimate fear is of death. This is not quite true. What we actually fear is the process of dying, the passing into the unknown, alone. It is the final letting-go. We fear entering the unknown, our utter lack of control, our aloneness. Or perhaps it is the particular image of God that we have that causes fear. Belief in a Last Judgement can cause a dead-line anxiety: the fear that there will not be enough time to complete what we think God expects of us.

All our life is a process of letting-go. When we first made our appearance on Earth as babies, the world centred around us, we had no concept of anything other. Gradually we learned that life was all about relationships, of living, not for self, but for the 'other'. When we came to realise true happiness is found in 'being more fully' rather than in having more and more, we began intentionally to let go. The big let-go for most of us was experienced during the teenage of our children. We had to express our love for them by letting go, letting go what was dearest to us, letting them be themselves to shape their own lives.

The final let-go

The more accustomed we have become to letting go during our life – what the spiritual masters call 'detachment' – the easier will be that final letting go as we pass out of this world.

In *Measure for Measure* Shakespeare wrote that when we are prepared for death, life is sweeter. Mozart called death the key to unlocking the door to true happiness, while Carl Jung, the eminent Swiss psychologist, said that it is psychologically beneficial to have death as a goal towards which to strive.

Many of those who have had a near-death experience recount how the whole of their life flashed before them – the good moments and the bad. What matters at our moment of dying is not, as religious writers would have us believe, a moment of judgement when all our past failings are weighed against what good we have done, whilst all the angels of the heavenly court hold their breath to see which way the scales tip! The significance of our past at that moment – good as well as evil – is the degree of love it has engendered in us at the moment of our transition. That is all that matters: our ability to love and to be open to receive love.

The many out-of-the-body experiences being recounted these days, all testify to the same thing: that our mind, our consciousness has an existence apart from our physical brain. So we can think of our death as a transformation to another state of consciousness.

Sogyal Rinpoche, in his *Tibetan Book of Living and Dying*, suggests that: 'Perhaps the deepest reason why we are afraid of death is because we do not know who we are'. We rely on props for our identity: names, achievements, partners, family, friends, property, professional position, title, bank balance. All these are at the surface level of life, external to us. We would be helped in letting go of our reliance on these props if periodically we were able to escape the constant noise and ceaseless activity that characterize our life in the West. So many people today fear silence, stillness. It reveals their emptiness. We fear to look into ourselves. Meister Eckhart wrote: 'Nothing in creation is so like God as stillness'.

Those of us who regularly practise twice-daily meditation notice that our fear of death diminishes. This is because in meditation we are letting go control of our thoughts, allowing ourselves to enter an unplotted state of consciousness. To be in a state of meditation is to let go our awareness of time and space. It is to live the NOW moment, which will be our state after death, with no expectations, just being, experiencing the 'I am'. '"I exist" is the only permanent, self-evident experience of everyone' said the Indian sage Ramana Maharshi, 'nothing else is so self-evident as "I am". I am is reality. I am this or that is unreal. God exists in "I am" in everything and every being.'

Our Christ life

To the Colossians Paul wrote: 'Your real life is Christ' (3:4) and to the Philippians he wrote: 'The attitude you should have is the one that Jesus the Christ had' (2:5). That is not to say he expected us to become clones of Jesus of Nazareth. Jesus lived in a particular era, in a Jewish middle-eastern culture, with all the human limitations of his time and place. We are people of another period. To imitate Jesus' qualities is one thing, but to live as a Palestinian Jew of two thousand years ago is neither our calling nor our possibility. To be another Christ, a human manifestation of the Divine, as he recognized himself to be, is something else. We are each of us a human manifestation of the Divine but the extent to which we reflect that outwardly is the extent to which we recognise the fact and consequently are able, in proportion to that recognition, to draw on the Christ energies. Jesus had this recognition to the degree that he was able to say 'I and the Father are one' and consequently was able to exercise the divine energies to the highest degree possible for a human being.

To the Christian community in Rome Paul wrote: 'Let God transform you inwardly by a complete change of your mind' (12:2) – of your mindset, of your attitude.

7 An evolving relationship between human beings and between nations

S0 used are we to thinking of our neighbours being those in our immediate neighbourhood, those with whom we associate as person to person, that it is easy to take the command 'Love your neighbour as yourself' to be a very localised admonition. Today our world has grown so small that everyone of the six billion and more individuals on the planet has become our neighbour.

In front of me on my desk I always keep a globe. Not large; it is golf-ball size and plastic and semi-transparent. It is unlike the schoolroom globes of our childhood marking out the frontiers of countries and even of empires. I can see through its cloud layers to the lands and oceans of Mother Earth. It is our home planet as we first saw it on 17th February 1959 when the USA Vanguard II space probe sent us those incredible photographs from 'outside', as it were. We were seeing the most beautiful delicate object floating in space with its oceans and its forests and its deserts in blues and greens and browns. We looked at it in wonder, realising we were looking at 'home', the only home of the whole human race.

Apart from causing us to make a shift in our ecological consciousness from a utilitarian attitude towards lifeless material resources to perceiving the whole planet as a living organism, of which we humans are just one component, this new perception of Planet Earth surely had a profound effect on the human psyche. We began to talk of the 'global village' and to appreciate the interconnectedness of not only all human beings with one another but of each of us with every feature of creation on Earth. We are not a collection of independent tribes but all one interdependent family. We all sink or swim together. This is our family home. We just have to get along together. There is no alternative. Nevertheless, we react to this reality in one of two ways.

As we have already said in the last chapter, our two primary instincts are the survival instinct and the growth instinct. If the survival instinct predominates we react to danger – real or imagined – by destroying or debilitating the assumed threat. The other becomes an opposition: we polarize opposites. We see everything as either with us or against us.

With the growth instinct we tend to reconcile opposites. If we let go of the fear the growth instinct emerges. We then start to see shades of grey and colours. We accept differences as opportunities for growth. I do not feel threatened or jealous because you are more able than I in this particular field. I rejoice that as a member of the human family I will benefit from your ability.

Globalisation

'Globalisation' is a constantly recurring word these days to describe the process whereby individuals, groups and countries are becoming increasingly inter-related. The word is used differently according to one's concerns.

Through the eyes of commerce it speaks of the growth of the transnational corporations – Nike, Coca-Cola, McDonald's, Exxon Mobil, General Motors, for example – each having revenues greater than the combined economic output (GDP) of the forty-eight least developed countries. Aided by the treaties of the World Trade Organisation they are intent upon gaining still more power and control.

Then there is the growing networking of information worldwide. Microsoft, AOL, Yahoo, Vodaphone have become household names. In 1930 a three-minute trans-Atlantic telephone call cost over £100 in today's value: while now it costs just 15p. Only a few decades ago to obtain information on a particular subject might have meant travel to a specialised library, in another country even. Today with the World Wide Web information about almost any subject, anywhere in the world is instantly obtainable by everyone on a home computer. And the processing power of computers is increasing at a rate of 35% a year.

Cultural globalisation

The globalisation of culture is another aspect of our shrinking world. We travel more to visit peoples of other cultures. World tourism counted 260 million visitors in 1980 and 590 million in 1998 and is expected to rise to 1.6 billion by 2020. But we do not even have to travel. We now meet other cultures in our home towns, if not in person then in the plethora of ethnic restaurants. Increasing international migration means greater cultural contact between countries and people. A trip down the aisle of fruit and vegetables in our local supermarket is a tour of the Third World. Ideas, goods, people, money travel more, faster, cheaper and in greater quantities than ever before. Like it or not, it is now generally accepted that globalisation is an unstoppable force.

Through electronic banking between the globe's Stock Exchanges speculators gamble 1.5 trillion dollars each day. This too is 'globalisation'! The IMF (International Monetary Fund) stated in May 1997: 'Globalisation refers to the growing interdependencies of countries worldwide through the increasing volume and variety of cross-border transactions in goods and services, and of international capital flows; and also through the rapid and widespread diffusion of all kinds of technology'.

This is a very materialist definition. Fortunately a more human perspective was given at the Millennium Summit in September 2000 when the United Nations played host to the largest ever gathering of world leaders. Their Declaration states: 'We believe that the central challenge we face today is to ensure that globalisation becomes a positive force for all the world's people.'

God's design for our world

Can we see any connection between our increasing globalisation as described above and God's design for us earthlings that Jesus proclaimed in the metaphor of the Kingdom of God?

Contrary to what we often read in Church documents, Jesus did not 'inaugurate' the Kingdom of God – it was God's design from the first moment of creation (Ephesians 1:4). What Jesus did was to manifest it to us, in the first place by living the vision in his own person and secondly by announcing it to us. He manifested and taught the unity with the Divine which is to be the destiny of all humanity and towards which we are always evolving. What kind of unity is this to be? The kind of unity for which Jesus prayed at the Last Supper was the unity consciousness which he himself experienced: 'So that they may be one, just as you and I are one' (John 17:11).

Can we recognise in any aspects of today's globalisation a movement towards the fulfilment of that unity for which Jesus prayed?

Towards a kingdom unity

In order to discern the working out of God's design in our day, we might recognize the appearance of a number of features of globalisation as being indicative of an increasing unity of humanity.

At the level of religions, the features of globalisation that I mentioned above are causing us to become more aware of the richness and holiness of the followers of Eastern faiths – Hinduism, Buddhism, Sikhism – who now live among us. Through the recent opening up of dialogue, we are more aware of how their particular insights into the spiritual journey can enrich our own understanding of Christian revelation.

The World Wide Web, another contributor to globalisation, is unwittingly militating against the hierarchical structures of society and of our institutions. It is a great equaliser, ignoring time and distance. Anyone, anywhere, with no need to advertise their 'authority' can post their point of view on everyone else's screen. We become rightly alarmed when we learn that globalisation can mean that one semi-educated young man on a tiny island in the Philippines can sit at his computer, shut down whole networks and cost the world's business billions of dollars by putting the words 'I love you' on the Internet. He did just that!

This dissolving of hierarchical power is in keeping with the vision Jesus had for our mutual relationships as sisters and brothers with a common Father. This was his vision of the Kingdom society that he announced through not only what he said but demonstrated by his own relationships with people. (Matthew 22:2-10. 23:6-10. Mark 10:13-16, 42-45. 12:14. John 13:4-15)

Our Christian concerns are global

Today our concerns have become planetary. We have a concern for injustices practised in far-off countries, for the mass poverty in the Southern Hemisphere, for the suffering caused by natural disasters at the other side of the globe. We now feel personally concerned about these as never before.

What better example than the massive world-wide response of compassion for the grieving families and dispossessed survivors of the Tsunami disaster in December 2004. People of all nations, cultures and religions spontaneously gave money and belongings to be sent to the other side of the world, for many, to a country and a people of whom they knew nothing.

We are alarmed at the environmental effect on the whole of our planet by our misuse and plundering of the Earth's natural resources.

We have set up an International Court of Justice to ensure justice and the rule of law in international affairs.

The problems of refugees and asylum-seekers have become our own problems and it is on a world scale that we are challenged by the widening gap between the rich and the poor, of which, incidentally, one of the causes is economic globalisation.

All these concerns reflect Kingdom values.

Not a new concept

While most of us became aware of the phenomenon of globalisation only in the past two decades, Teilhard de Chardin was writing about it more than sixty years ago. He usually referred to it as 'planetisation' or sometimes as 'hominisation of the planet'. He wrote: 'No evolutionary future awaits human beings except in association with all other human beings'. He foresaw our future as a new level of (world-wide) human society – the super-society – which would experience an even higher level of consciousness, a corporate or global consciousness. This is not just a sociological feature. It is a spiritual matter. At least it is if we are able to recognise what is happening in our world as a great move forward towards that unity for which Jesus prayed: a step nearer to his vision becoming a reality.

Our assumptions are changing

In their book *Breaking Through* Walter and Dorothy Schwarz list some of the assumptions upon which our civilisation has been based over the last two centuries and which are challenged today by the shift in consciousness that is taking place. These are:

> That large organisations (firms, government departments, schools, etc) are more effective than smaller ones.
> That an essential purpose of an economic system is to provide at least one full-time paid job for every household.
> That an economy, however large, can only prosper if it continues to grow.
> That industrial societies provide the most promising model for the rest of the world.
> That economic aid enables the Third World to develop.
> That the principal purpose of education is to open the way to a full-time paid job for life.
> That the best way to a healthier society is to provide more hospitals, more doctors and more medical machines.

That the earth is an unlimited source of raw materials and an infinite receptacle for waste.

That one country's economy and ecology can be kept separate from another's.

That knowledge is only valid if it is scientifically proven.

That emotion is a less valid criterion for action than reason.

That God is male.

Against this, John Naisbitt highlights the shift taking place in our present society. In his book *Megatrends* he identifies ten significant trends currently transforming our lives. He shows where we are coming from and the characteristics of the society towards which we are heading. The chapter headings of his book list them thus:

FROM	TO
Industrial society	Information society
Forced technology	High Tech/High Touch (meaning counterbalancing human response)
National economy	World economy
Short-term	Long-term
Centralisation	Decentralisation
Institutional help	Self-help
Representative democracy	Participatory democracy
Hierarchies	Networking
North	South
Either/or	Multiple option

Decide to network

The globalisation of our planet means that each of us can become an instrument of unity-building far more effectively than we ever could in the past. Our means is by *networking*. We are now able to link up with others, world-wide, who have the same vision and concerns as ourselves. Networking is the new power we all have to bring about change in our world; a strategy for co-operation and creative inter-communication. Formally, the initiative for change was taken by those at the peak of the human pyramid. That was where power was. Today power is being exercised at grassroots: people power. It is being exercised by ordinary folk linking up to share ideas and initiate action. Networkers have no central command post nor leaders who issue orders. They are self-actualising people. Networkers are the 'unorganisers' of tomorrow, the de-centralisers. They provide a cross-disciplinary approach to people and issues.

It has been rightly claimed that there are two super-powers influencing our world today: the United States of America and People-power.

I close this chapter with the wise advice of Dr. Robert Muller when he was Assistant Secretary General of the United Nations.

Use every letter you write
Every conversation you have
Every meeting you attend
To express your fundamental beliefs and dreams
Affirm to others the vision of the world you want
Network through thought
Network through action
Network through love
Network through the spirit
You are the centre of a network
You are the centre of the world
You are a free, immensely powerful source of life and goodness
Affirm it
Spread it
Radiate it
Think day and night about it
And you will see a miracle happen:
the greatness of your own life.
In a world of big powers, media and monopolies
But of six and a half billion individuals
Networking is the new freedom
the new democracy
A new form of happiness.

8 An evolving relationship between humanity, our planet and the universe

WHEN the Polish astronomer Copernicus published his epoch-making work *On the Revolution of the Heavenly Spheres* in 1543 it was judged heresy by the Church. It contradicted the theologians' Scriptural understanding that humanity is the perfection of, and indeed the very reason for the whole of creation. Besides, it was self-evident every morning and evening, that the Sun travelled round the Earth. Such a ridiculous theory, had to be condemned. His works were placed on the Papal Index of forbidden books. His personal fate might have been the same as that of Galileo, had he not died just after the publication of his work.

Less known is the fact that churchmen were not the only opponents of his theory. The 'scientists' of the day also felt threatened. (The designation *scientist* was coined by William Whewell only in 1840. Previously, such men as Galileo, Newton and Bacon were known as 'philosophers of nature' – of the natural world – as differing from the philosophers of logic and reason.) Even up to 1600 there were very few among them who were able to make the tremendous psychological shift in recognising that the Sun was the centre point of our solar system, the then known Universe.

The Copernicus revelation was the entry into a new epoch. It shattered a world view that had been held from the earliest days when human beings first gave thought to such matters. For our ancestors the world, our planet, was the only known reality. Little was known about the stars. To the Egyptians they were the presence of their gods and goddesses and the spirits of past Pharaohs. To the astrologers of Persia stars were signs and omens revealing future events. When St Paul speaks of the Christ in universal terms – that the redemptive act of Jesus had a cosmic effect – it is with the limited cosmology of his day: 'Through the Son, God decided to bring the whole Universe back to Himself. God made peace through His Son's death on the cross and so brought back to Himself all things both on Earth and in Heaven' (Colossians 1:20).

A second epochal breakthrough

The discovery in the last century by Edwin Hubble, the American astronomer, that we are part of an ever-expanding Universe and that the more distant the galaxy, the greater the speed with which it is receding, is equally epoch-making. This discovery too has met with resistance, notably from Einstein. Even Hubble himself took some years to accept all the implications of the data he was receiving from his telescope.

It is beyond the comprehension of most of us that we have to say today that the Universe has no central point, there is no above or below. Relatively speaking, each of us is our own centre point of the Universe.

The Universe is all one. It is our perception that divides it. We deal with it in parts and give those parts names. In doing so we lose sight of the interconnectedness of the whole.

Accepting that the Universe is continually expanding, if we run the film backwards, so to speak, we see it continually contracting until we arrive at that initial explosion of energy from which it all came about: the Big Bang, as another eminent scientist, Sir Fred Hoyle, derisively called it. Hoyle is not the only scientist unwilling to embrace the Big Bang theory, because it faces them with a question which is beyond the remit of science, a theological question: who or what caused the Big Bang?

The answer to such a question lies beyond our imagination because there was no *before* the Big Bang and we are unable to imagine timelessness. Time, as we have said, is an object of our creation. Even a theologian 1,500 years ago arrived at this understanding long before our scientists! St Augustine of Hippo (354-430) wrote:

> It is idle to look for time before creation, as if time can be found before time. If there was no motion of either a spiritual or a corporeal creature by which the future, moving through the present, would succeed the past, there would be no time at all. ... We should therefore say that time began with creation, rather than that creation began with time.

It makes no sense, then, to think of God 'pre-dating' the Universe. The God we can know can only be known in the manifestations of that primal energy.

Today there is taking place another great shift in our thinking about our place in the Universe.

As I remarked at the beginning of Chapter 7, those incredible photographs of Planet Earth sent back by the space-probe Vanguard II in February 1959, opened our eyes not only to the beauty of our planet but also to its insignificance – and our personal insignificance – against the vastness of the total Universe. It is hard to accept how tiny Earth is in the total picture. To accept that Earth is only one of nine planets (or have astronomers now discovered a tenth?) revolving around one star, our Sun, and not a very significant planet at that: it is neither the largest nor the smallest, it is not the hottest nor the coldest. But it is just right for us! Furthermore, there are 100 billion other stars in the galaxy we call the Milky Way. Every year we discover that more of them also have their planets revolving around them. And if that outlook is not vast enough, let us remind ourselves that there are at least 100 billion other galaxies beyond ours. To look at our own planets on a clear night is to look back into the past. When we see Saturn we are seeing it as it was one and a half hours ago. Even the light from our Sun takes eight minutes to reach us, with light travelling at a speed of 300,000 kilometres per second. Our nearest star in the Milky Way we have named Proxima Centauri. What we are seeing is its light as it was four years ago. It is 400 trillion kilometres away. We see the furthest galaxy as it was eleven billion years ago, which was not so long after the Big Bang, fifteen billion years ago.

This is the adjustment we have to make to our relationship with our planet looking 'outwards', so to speak.

But let us concentrate on our own planet. Looking after our Earth is going to take all our energies and intelligence, for we alone, of all creatures, have a responsibility for its future. It is home for over six billion of us, as it is home for millions of different species of living creatures. We need to give it our full attention!

Looking inwards

The direction to which we must look in order to relate in a realistic way to our planet, is inwards. I identify four major eras in which this relationship has changed.

The first is the pre-agricultural, pre-animal husbandry period. For thousands of years, even millions may be, our ancestors lived in harmony with the Earth. Their life was governed by its natural rhythms and seasons, and the Earth was worshipped as the great goddess, the source of life and fertility. The inability of these early ancestors to explain or control the mysterious phenomena of nature, gave rise to their imagining a class of powerful but unseen beings, gods or spirits, whom they had to humour.

Then, some 12,000 years ago we became agriculturists. Our consciousness had developed to the point where an understanding of past and future became features of life. By planting today food would become available at a later date. The earth was being put to use. This required that land be possessed and possessiveness of land led to exploitation, appropriation and warfare. The fertility goddess was replaced by the male god of domination and war. Societies, always growing into larger and larger units, became hierarchical. They also became patriarchal. Fighting to defend or gain territory was male business. With land being possessed personally, the few became rich, the many became dependent upon them.

The third era of changed relationship between human beings and our Earth, at least in the West, was with the spread of Christendom over the first millennium, during which the Earth was regarded as 'no abiding city'. Life was about struggling to enter Heaven. The Earth was relegated to a secondary value, a means to that end. The spiritual was more important than the material: our souls more important than our bodies. Medieval theologians, such as the great St Thomas Aquinas, valued the Earth as no more than an object to be used to help us reach our eternal destiny in another place.

We can be mistaken in thinking that this understanding of our relationship to the Earth has its roots in the New Testament use of the word 'world', if we consider only some passages of Johannine writing. For instance, in the First Letter of John we read: 'Do not love the world or anything that belongs to the world' (2:15) and in the Gospel of John Jesus is often reported as speaking about himself and his followers as not being 'of the world'. This is but one understanding of 'the world', which issues from a Gnostic influence, opposing evil (the material created world) to good (the spirit), and belief that our spiritual dimension was held in bondage by the material. But John also uses 'the world' to mean all of humanity, as when the Gospel records Jesus saying: 'God loved the world so much that he gave His only son, so that everyone who believes in him may not die but have eternal life' (3:16).

The last millennium saw a reversal of these values. Rationalism, the Enlightenment, the birth of science discarded the spiritual in favour of the here-and-now, the 'real', the evident. Our Earth was for our use. Not now as a means of gaining a higher life but as a means of providing a materially richer life.

Human attitudes towards the Earth over the last two eras caused our present day dualistic thinking. We in the West live in two realms: the material and the spiritual. We set up an opposition between the profane and the holy, between nature and grace, between human and divine. In our Upper House of Parliament we speak of the Lords Spiritual (referring to the Bishops) and the Lords Temporal. The presumption behind such dualistic thinking is that if the spiritual is of primary importance, the material can endanger it. This duality is reflected in our everyday spirituality where on the one side is day-to-day business, while on the other, the spirit is attended to with occasional prayer, even more occasional fasting and Sunday worship. This is world denying. It implies an unreality about this world as just a place of passage on our way to the 'real' world of the 'next life'.

Today this attitude is changing. We are becoming 'this-worldly', appreciating natural beauty, the body and sex for themselves. There is less willingness to embrace those ascetic practices which are body-denying. There is evident dissatisfaction with the classical religious practices which separate body and soul. We no longer accept that a small group of religious leaders should hold our passports to the next life.

Into the third millennium

I believe our new millennium is a time for bringing together the values of the two previous millennia. The discarded world of the first millennium and the discarded soul of the second are being brought into the same equation. Between the first and second millennia we had moved from a predominantly right-brain outlook of magic and symbol and myth to a left-brain approach to our world where our rational, critical faculties predominated, developing our secularisation, our autonomy and our individualism. Now there are signs that we are re-awakening to a synthesis at a higher level of consciousness, to a balance of left and right brain, to a spiritual interpretation of reality.

The Jesuit palaeontologist, Teilhard de Chardin, provides an interesting illustration of humanity's relationship with the world over the millennia. Let us imagine, he says, that a pulsation enters the planet at the South Pole and spreads slowly Northwards. There are two phases in such a progression. From the Pole to the Equator there is a gradual expansion. This represents humanity spreading from its origins in East Africa throughout the whole world. On account of this expansion the pressure was low which accounts for the advance of socialisation being extremely slow, a gradual branching out into various races and tribes. The second phase of the pulse's journey is from the expanse of the Equator to the concentrated point of the North Pole. All available space on Earth began to be occupied and waves of human socialisation began to interpenetrate. Humanity began to pack together more tightly into larger and larger conurbations. This has led to our sharing each other's thoughts to a greater and greater degree. This is what has led to our modern technological revolution. We have now come to constitute, he says, an almost solid mass of humanity. We are experiencing the phase of contraction, of convergence. Teilhard calls this contemporary trend 'Planetisation', the emergence of a global consciousness.

Our interdependence

While appreciating that we are Earthlings, the only species to be spread over the entire surface of this planet, the only species able to exercise any form of control over our environment, we are becoming more appreciative that we are not over and above nature as little gods dominating lesser species, but are just one of the millions of species with which we share the Earth. Because we have the faculty of choice to decide how we relate to our planet – and in this we differ from all other species – does not mean that we are more important to the whole than any other. Our growing realisation of the interdependence of all creatures 'puts us in our place'. I am no more important to the planet than the blackbird presently singing outside my window or the tree which is casting its shadow over my desk.

Just how puny we human beings are in the face of nature's forces was brought home to us on Boxing Day 2004 when witnessing the horrific widespread effect of the Tsunami, the tidal wave caused by the earthquake in the Indian ocean. Despite our scientific and technological advances we are not, as we would like to think, in control of our environment. The ancient Greeks would have told us that Gaia, Goddess Earth, is in charge of Earth. We have to know our place and treat her with the greatest respect.

In one crucial way we differ from all other creatures. We are the only animals on the planet able to make choices. This has two consequences. In the first place, we are able to make wrong or less perfect, less fully human choices and so suffer the consequences. The rest of the animal world being unable to choose, cannot make mistakes. What they do is always right because it always follows their nature. Sadly, however, they also bear the consequences of the wrong choices of humans.

A second consequence of our ability to choose is our need to ask questions. Where are we heading? What good or bad will come of this? Who is to tell us? Life has no meaning of itself: it just is. It is we who give it meaning. The meaning we give it is going to be derived either from experience or from what Christian tradition calls 'divine revelation'. If we subscribe to the latter then we are going to believe that answers are provided – injected into our intuition, so to speak – by an outside agent whom we in the West name 'God'.

Before science came into its own, our ancestors believed they lived in a ready-made cosmos, specially designed to be a home for human beings and with an in-built moral order. The alternative view, basing our answer to life's meaning on experience, finds only mathematical patterns in the world, not a given moral order. We are the creators of the moral order by which we live.

If we choose an exterior God to provide our answers we are in the realm of faith and have to take on board all the baggage of the beliefs of a particular religion, with all its emotional consequences. This involves having to relate what we experience as reality to the myth, and with our knowledge of the Universe increasing, constant adjustments have to be made. It has been a traditional belief of Christians that God created everything directly. A first adjustment was made, not so long ago, when Christians had to give up a literal belief in the Genesis account of creation in six days. Now a further adjustment is being made. Christians are accepting that different species came about by evolution, yes, even we humans. And that it took billions of years of evolution to produce the human species. However, while allowing that our physical bodies have evolved, there is still the faith belief that the soul of each of us is directly created by God. For instance, the *Catechism of the Catholic Church* (n.366) states: 'The Church teaches that every spiritual soul is created immediately by God – it is not "produced" by the parents'. The implication is that in the eye of the Creator we are more special than and superior to any other creature. This maintains the anthropological paradigm (that we human beings are at the centre and that everything revolves around us) and a hierarchical order in creation. Astonishingly, the same Catechism says: 'The hierarchy of creatures is expressed by the order of the "six days" [of creation], from the less perfect to the more perfect' (n.342) and 'Man is the summit of the Creator's work' (n.343).

Deep ecology

The two ways of regarding our relationship with the Earth which I have described above, are set out by the Norwegian philosopher Arne Naess in terms of Shallow Ecology and Deep Ecology. By the former he refers to the traditional Newtonian world view (shared by the Catholic Catechism) in which everything was understood as human-centred. In this perspective humanity is outside and above the rest of nature because we consider ourselves as the pinnacle of creation, the most superb of all creatures. We perceive everything else as having a value only in relation to us and their value is a *use* value: how useful this or that is for us.

By Deep Ecology, on the other hand, he understands humanity as being part of the total natural environment. All living beings, and the non-living too, have the same intrinsic value. All have a part to play. Everything in nature, as we have already seen, is interconnected and interdependent.

Gradually today more people are moving into the Deep Ecology relationship with our planet. To make such a mental shift is to make a shift also in the manner in which we treat the Earth. As the only creatures with a free will and a sense of past and future we have a unique responsibility for the future of our planet. Response-ability: the ability to respond to the pulse of life around us. This is to come to a new understanding of the words Christians recite daily in the Lord's prayer: 'thy Kingdom come thy will be done on Earth as it is in Heaven'. May this Earth become the harmonious place that was the vision of Jesus who saw not only humanity but all of creation radiating Divine Being.

9 An evolving relationship with the transcendent

H UMANITY'S relationship with the Divine is always evolving as a consequence of the evolution of human consciousness.

To understand our first humanity-God relationship we have to go back to the evolutionary event when our earliest ancestors broke out of a state of non-differential unity, described in our Scripture as the Eden-state, to seeking a unity in our diversity. What signified our evolution from *homo erectus* to *homo sapiens* was the new ability to be self-reflective, to be able to experience the gap between Self and Other. In Hebrew scripture this is portrayed as an emergence from that Eden-state. It was a new form of knowing, of realising that I am not that other. Till then those early ancestors had experienced a unity without differentiation between I and the other. This was a necessary evolutionary leap in order to develop, to become more fully human. It was the first step on a journey towards a different experience of unity: unity with differentiation. Sadly, in Hebrew Scripture this tremendous break-through in our progress towards becoming more fully human is depicted negatively as a banishment from the bliss of the Garden of Eden. But it was a necessity. It had to happen if we were to develop a higher level of consciousness.

Traditionally, Christians have been persuaded that it was a 'Fall', a retrograde step, an evil from which humanity had to be redeemed.

With a careful look at the Genesis text it will be noticed that there is no mention of a Fall, nor even that the act of Adam and Eve is described as sinful.

The evolutionary step out of the Garden of Eden finds its parallel in the evolutionary step that each of us took in our entry into the world. The months we spent in our mother's womb was our time in the Eden-state. We were not self-aware. We were one with our mother, unaware of being different from our mother. It was a glorious time: we were warm, fed, cared for, protected from outside interference. It was a veritable Eden! But to have attempted to survive in that state for ever would have arrested our development. It would have meant death. Neither could humanity survive in the Eden-state for ever. The force of evolution thrust both humanity as a whole, and our own embryonic selves, into a new world. We met our personal 'Fall'. We cried and screamed at this separation, at being expelled into a cold, threatening world. We gradually began to experience that there was a gap between ourselves and other persons and things: that we are separate beings. This had to happen. To resist the force of evolution is to invite death.

Discovering space and time

The experience of separation by the evolving *homo sapiens* led to the new experience of space. There was space between me and others. Similarly there grew an experience of time, which is space in a different dimension. I am separate from what went before, so there must also be a 'what is to come'.

As newly born babies we discovered that if we are separate from other people, we have to relate to them in order to survive. Nature provides the baby with the first tool for self-survival – a foghorn! – and she soon becomes adept at using this to have her needs met.

The experience of our early ancestors of separation from other people led to the experience that there was a separation of wills. Others thought differently, they did things differently. There was friction, there was anger, there was pain inflicted by others. Our ability to be reflective caused pain to become suffering. Human beings, alone of all creatures, suffer. Suffering is caused by our reflection on pain and only creatures with a sense of time are able to suffer. It is our experience of time, not of pain, that is the cause of our suffering. Animals feel pain but they do not suffer because they live in the immediacy of the present moment. Unlike us they cannot ask themselves: 'How long is this going to last? Can I endure it any further? How did I get over it last time?'

The new sense of time, of space, of suffering caused our early ancestors to look for the means to deal with them. Once separate from nature, they had to deal with nature. How to find food, how to keep warm – or cool, as the case may be – how to live peacefully together. So much was beyond their physical power to deal with their environment, that they had to invoke higher, transcendent powers, in whatever form. The concept of a spirit world emerged. So began rituals, sacrifices, charms, and the need of a go-between, the shaman. We can call this the birth of religion. There was no original primal truth which humanity lost. Religion began as a tribal awareness. It held together the values of the tribe but it was also the seed of conflict between tribes. (As still in our own day different religious views are at the heart of so much cultural conflict.)

The shaman

A channel of communication with the spirit world was required in order to tap into its resources to fulfil the needs that these primitive human beings could not satisfy by their own power. Those among them who manifested some special gift or power or mystery were appointed to be that go-between, the shaman. So shamans became medicine men (or women), visionaries, leaders of rituals and guides to the world beyond the senses. With incantations and spells they assisted the tribe in the hunt and strengthened them for battle. Evidence of their early existence in Europe can be found in the cave paintings at Lascaux, Pech-merle and Les Trois Frere, painted more than 20,000 years ago, and in the Drakensberg mountains of South Africa going back 25,000 years. They depict people going into a trance and hallucinating as a means of bringing together the spirit world and our own world.

Discoveries in Siberia, Africa, Central Asia, Australia and North and South America show remarkable similarities between shamanistic practices in different parts of the world. Their clients believed that by their entering into a trance they travelled to the heavens and the underworld to communicate with the ancestors and supernatural beings. Having such powers they were best placed to preside over the rites of passage: birth, adolescent initiation, marriage and death. They were the forerunners of those intermediaries with the Transcendent better known to us: the prophets, the saints, the priests.

The Hebrew prophets

It is beyond the scope of this book to trace the whole development of the relationship between humanity and the Transcendent throughout our human history and through different cultures. Gradually religions became imperial – Chinese, Byzantine, Roman, Egyptian – dominating local cultures. However, there is one culture which, in this respect, has had a profound influence on us in the West for two and a half thousand years, and continues to have: that of the Hebrews.

Right across Asia and the Middle East, between 600 and 300 BCE there was an extraordinary intellectual evolution taking place, accompanied by spiritual creativity. It was the period when emerged the Vedic science in India, Taoism in China, the spread of Buddhism, the work of the Greek philosophers, Pythagoras, Socrates, Plato and Aristotle. This period saw such a shift in human consciousness that it caused human culture to take a giant turn on its axis. As we said in Chapter 1 it has come to be referred to as the 'Axial Age'.

Among the great minds of that period were the Hebrew Prophets. They are usually divided between Major and Minor prophets, more on account of the length of their writings in Scripture than on account of the influence they had on their fellow Jews. They laid the foundation of the relationship between humanity and the Divine in western culture, expressed first in Judaism and later in Christianity and later still in Islam. They shifted their culture from the polytheism of previous cultures to monotheism. They bequeathed to us two major advances in thoughts about God and His purposes. The one I would describe as helpful, the other, at least as regards our present-day knowledge, as unhelpful.

Humanity has a direction

Most cultures at the time of the Hebrew prophets, such as the ancient Greek and the Eastern religions, regarded life as cyclic. Not only were individual lives cyclic, through reincarnation in some form, but history as a whole. For Hindus the complete cycle is called Manvantara and it is divided into four immensely long periods of time, or 'Yugas'. The first is the Golden Age (Krita Yuga) which gradually deteriorates into the next less-golden age, half its length (Treta Yuga) which in turn gives way to a less perfect age still, the Dvapara Yuga, and finally the shortest age of all and the least perfect, the Iron Age (Kali Yuga) which we are in at present. Some idea can be had of the length of these cycles when one learns that our present age (and each is half the length of the previous age) is said to have a duration of 432,000 years!

The insight of the Jewish people was to perceive their own history as linear. There was a beginning, described mythologically in the six days of creation, and their lives were being led forward. They saw this as applying to themselves as a nation. Their God was active in their history, leading them forward with a purpose. This linear appreciation of history was absorbed into Christianity. St Augustine of Hippo (354-430) suggested that while all species had been created by God in the Beginning, some were mere seeds that would appear at a later time. In Christian belief the 'end' is described as the Parusia, or the final coming of the Christ when he will hand over his Kingdom to his Father (I Corinthians 15:24).

Since the mid-nineteenth century, with the discoveries of Charles Darwin and Alfred Wallace, and their theory of species evolving, science has given its support to the linear concept. The theory of evolution is now so widely held that it is doubted by very few, mostly by the Creationists who feel more at ease with a literal understanding of the first chapters of the Bible. Not all evolutionists are in agreement with Darwin's explanation of natural selection and the 'survival of the fittest' as the motivation behind species evolving. Nor would they all agree with the theory that evolution has occurred as a single smooth progression. But the more we discover from fossils and the further back in time we can peer into the origins of our solar system and of the Universe itself, the more we must accept that there has been – at least on Planet Earth – a progression of development to more and more complex organisms, an unfolding process of living things.

We human beings consider ourselves as the latest, most complex product of the evolutionary process and in doing so risk believing we are the final stage, the ultimate purpose of creation; that all the steps that went before, over the fifteen billion years since the Big Bang, were no more than necessary steps for the appearance on Earth of what God really wanted: a human being who could reflect upon herself and claim to be 'made in the image of God'. What incredible arrogance! What reason have we to believe that the evolutionary energy will not cause further development of our species? As we shall see in the next chapter, there is evidence in our present times that humanity is moving into a higher state of consciousness.

God: an all-powerful being

The other, and less helpful, contribution that the Hebrew Prophets made to Western culture was to bequeath us a particular model of the Transcendent: the perception of the Divine, as a larger-than-human Being. A 'someone' like us with all our attributes and faculties, but more so, to the degree of perfection. If we have an experience of Truth, Love, Justice, Goodness, Beauty, Mercy and all the other virtues, we think of God as Someone possessing them to an infinite degree. So both Hebrew Scripture and our own New Testament present a God who cares, who loves, who guides, who gives us laws to live by and even who punishes us for transgressing them.

Whether this God is so majestic and mighty that His name cannot be uttered by the Jews of Jesus' time or whether He can be related to as a caring loving Father, the fundamental concept is the same: of *a*

Being in contrast to all created beings. Bishop John Spong in his book *A New Christianity for a New World* expresses very clearly that while a perception of the Divine as *a* Being, *a* Person, has been helpful to our ancestors over the last four thousand years, such imagery does not speak to today's generation who have quite a different way of perceiving reality and Ultimate Reality. He names this imagery 'a theistic deity' which he defines as 'a being, supernatural in power, dwelling outside this world and invading the world periodically to accomplish the Divine Will'. With the continued use today of hymns and prayers and sermons which enforce the God imagery of antiquity, most people fall back on this imagery in moments of crisis. How often we hear mature adults ending their recital of some accident they narrowly escaped with the words: 'Someone up there was looking after me'. Even though such an image is in contradiction with everyday life as they experience it, they believe they can influence God by their prayer: even have God change His mind!

Because God is in all His love permeates us, but we are blind to it. God's mercy surrounds us, we don't have to keep asking for it – but when we do we are reminded of it. We ask for forgiveness but we are already forgiven. All that happens during those lengthy prayers we say is that they help to focus our minds on how immersed in the Divine we already are.

On the same plane is the belief that we can give God something He has not got, add to His glory, to His happiness by our good deeds, our prayers of praise, our worship, our sacrifices.

Everything we think *about* God, every name and quality we give to God is a creation of the human mind.

The birth of the theistic God goes right back to that stage of evolution when human beings realised their separateness from one another, from their surroundings. They had to act upon their surroundings in order to survive. They had only their hands and primitive tools. They had no fire, no way of dealing with their environment. As we saw earlier, all they could do was to appeal to some greater, outer, unknown force to act on their behalf. Thus gradually emerged the idea of an all-powerful Divine Being out there who controlled their lives and assisted them to survive. As humanity evolved and became more technically competent, so did its concept of the role of God in human life change. The idea, the explanation, of a God out there is being seen by many people now as a human creation to enable humanity to cope with the fears and needs of daily life in harsh surroundings. Long ago the Roman poet Lucretius (c99-55BCE) put this succinctly: 'Fear was the first thing on earth to make gods'. We create a God who reflects our own desires and supplies for our limitations. We can do no other as long as our God is outside us, separate from us. Xenophanes, a Greek philosopher (500 BCE) wrote that if horses had hands they would draw pictures of the gods looking like horses. Horses have horsey limitations as we have our human limitations. This God of our imagination answers a deep human need to relate to a higher Other.

God: from noun to verb

People are regarding our present times as a human coming-of-age. We are technological people having less recourse to outside intervention to satisfy our needs and accomplish what we desire. Nevertheless, vestiges of this notion of a rescuing God are deep within us. When people, who would not describe themselves as religious, become victims of accidents or threatened by a natural disaster, they 'turn to religion' in their desperation: they turn to a power beyond the Universe, their last resort.

The traditional concept began to be challenged by theologians of the last century, such as Dietrich Bonhoeffer, Rudolf Bultmann, Paul Tillich and our own John Robinson in his 1963 tradition-shattering book *Honest to God.*

The big picture we have of the world today and of our place in it, enables us to move from the concept of God as a supernatural Being, a concept that holds us in a child-parent relationship, to experience the Divine as 'Being'. I am using the word 'Being' as a verb, not as a noun. God is Being. We are human-Being, that is, expressions of being in created time-space form. God is a verb.*

---

* I have devoted a book to the changing perception of the Divine Mystery: *The God Shift*.

A mystic of the Middle Ages, St Bernard of Clairvaux (1090-1153) wrote: 'Who is God? I can think of no better answer than He who is. Nothing is more appropriate to the eternity which God is. If you call God good or blessed or wise, or anything else of this sort, it is included in these words, namely, He is'.

To say, as I did earlier, that the image of a transcendent Being is a creation of the human mind on account of the human inability to manage the circumstances of life, is not to deny the existence of the Transcendent. As we create images of the unimaginable so we name the un-nameable. This was neatly expressed by Meister Eckhart, another mystic of the Middle Ages, in making the distinction between the Godhead (the Transcendent) and God. This latter is the Divine brought down to our human size as *a* Being we can think about and relate to and depend upon – the theistic God.

In our own time the theologian Paul Tillich makes the distinction between God and what he names 'the God-beyond-God': God immanent and God transcendent. Similarly, Hindus distinguish between God manifest and God unmanifest, or the Relative and the Absolute.

An illustration might help. After all, the best we can do is to work with images. Compare the Absolute to the limitless ocean of life, silent and existing always in the same state. Waves represent the Relative, the different aspects of creation, ever changing. When we look at the ocean we do not see it in its entirety. It is too vast for that. We see its expression in the waves at the surface. Each of us, and all matter around us, are like waves on the surface of the ocean. Each is distinct yet part of the whole, of the Absolute, of the unlimited vastness of pure existence. As waves we are in movement, in space and time, yet without the ocean we would have no existence. We are the outer expression of the inner Ultimate Reality. We relate to other waves. We are visible only on the surface. Each wave is different. The wave has a time-limited existence. It forms out at sea, travels towards the shore and disappears. It manifests and imparts the energy of the ocean itself – especially to surfers!

Despite the title of this chapter, I am not advocating a new relationship with the Absolute whom we name God, but rather an evolving perception of God which is more in accord with our advances in psychology and technology. 'Being' whom we depend upon less to make up for our own inabilities and shortcomings but, at the same time, Being as the Ground of all that is.

God is now

God understood as Being (verb) exists always in the present moment. I said earlier that when our ancestors began to differentiate themselves from the other, they acquired a sense of space and time. Time is a product of our creative mind. The only reality is the present moment, the NOW moment. As we saw in Chapter 6, there is no such reality as *the* past; there is only our memory of what went before. It has existence only with our giving it thought at this present moment. Similarly, there is no such thing as *the* future. Our imagination at this present moment foresees what we expect to happen next. Both past and future are human projections, projected either backwards in memory or forwards in anticipation from the present moment. The NOW moment is the only reality, our most natural, indeed our only state. It is the only moment I am really Me.

The NOW moment is our contact moment with the Absolute, the Divine. Life is NOW. In the NOW we become a bridge between the Absolute and the Relative, between God and creation.

In the NOW moment of God, everything is held in existence and given the energy to evolve.

Everyone of us continues to exist from moment to moment by this same creative energy. All is from God. There is no other source. All is *of* God. There is no other independent being. The Eastern religions express this literally in saying that everything that exists *is* God and God *is* everything that exists. We name this belief *pantheism*. Accordingly, our final goal is to lose our identity by being absorbed into God. The monotheistic religions of the West (Judaism, Christianity and Islam) maintain a separation between the Creator and the creature, and so our final destiny is to be united *with* not absorbed *into* God. We will retain our identity. Some theologians today have bridged the two notions by coining the word *panentheism*: we are *in* God and God is *in* us. Marcus Borg, professor of Religion and Culture at Oregon State University, USA, in his book *The God we Never Knew* writes: 'Panentheism – because it affirms both the transcendence and immanence of God – seems to me to be the orthodox Christian root concept of God, even though the notion is not widely known in popular Christianity'.

10 The climate of our new society: an emerging spirituality

A T a seminar I was leading recently one of the participants offered a succinct definition of spirituality: 'the effect the inner person has on the outer'! Spirituality is related to the vision we have of the person we wish to become. For many today who seek a meaning for their lives, what they label as 'spirituality' is giving them a direction: it is offering a vision of what could be.

It is important to distinguish spirituality from religion. Over the last decade I have been working with a great many groups on areas of spirituality. I have always asked them what they mean by that word because it is so widely used these days to cover so many different experiences from candles round the bath to the reading of Tarot cards, from spiritual channelling to Tai Chi.

Unlike religion, which, as we have seen arose from the need to invoke the help of unseen powers to deal with the challenges of life, spirituality is innate to the human person, disposing us towards finding a meaning in life. It transcends religion. Putting together the main ideas that are voiced in these groups, I have attempted to create what is no more than a working definition. One cannot do more because spirituality is concerned with mystery. Here it is.

> *Spirituality* is that dimension of our nature – related to the physical and psychological dimensions – which awakens us to

wonder, gives our lives meaning and calls us towards our higher self, usually expressed as a relationship with the Transcendent (sometimes named 'God').

Religion, on the other hand, which has been a feature of only recent history – for little over three thousand years of the million or so years of human existence – is a particular framework which includes four characteristics (a belief system, a moral code, an authority structure and a form of ritual) within which people find direction and nourishment for the spiritual dimension of their lives, and explore their spiritual journey in the company of others.

The most complete description I have found of what people today mean by 'spirituality' is provided by U. Thant, the former Secretary General of the United Nations:

> Spirituality is a state of connectedness to life.
>
> It is an experience of being, belonging and caring.
>
> It is sensitivity and compassion, joy and hope.
>
> It is the harmony between the innermost life and the outer life, or the life of the world and the life universal.
>
> It is the supreme comprehension of life in time and space, the tuning of the inner person with the great mysteries and secrets that are around us.
>
> It is the belief in the goodness of life and the possibility for each person to contribute goodness to it.
>
> It is the belief in life as part of the eternal stream of time, that each of us came from somewhere, that without such belief there could be no prayer, no meditation, no peace and no happiness.

If that describes spirituality in the broadest sense, we notice that particular expressions of it are emerging today.

What is emerging today?

We notice a multi-faceted phenomenon to which the media have applied the label *The New Age Movement.* The label is used to cover such a wide variety of human interests, speculations, theories and activities that a Christian might well be tempted to reject the whole scene as something godless. Indeed, some do. But this 'whole scene' is so complex that it is easier to start by saying what this phenomenon is not rather than what it is.

It is called a *movement* only in the sense that it is a growing feature of western culture, aspects of it attracting increasingly more people, but not because there is any particular organisation promoting it or any development policy being pursued. (For this reason I prefer to call it a trend.) It was not launched upon the world by a single event. There are no leaders, there is no hierarchical structure. There is no unifying ideology, no dogma nor any accepted body of authoritative texts. There are no headquarters nor membership. It is not a religion although some people may give it a quasi-religious value.

Vague though the phenomenon might seem, one thing we cannot properly do is to ignore the whole scene. In the '60s and '70s it was just a fringe concern of a few people we labelled 'weird' and it came to our attention only as 'something coming out of California' associated with flower power or as Summer solstice celebrations. It did not really intrude upon our everyday lives. Its principal characteristic in those decades was personal development.

More recently, what was decidedly marginal, has emerged as a contemporary sub-culture arousing the interest, and often involvement, of 'respectable' people, perhaps our friends among them. If not ourselves, do we not know people who have benefited from acupuncture or reflexology, who have become vegetarians and give their custom to whole-food shops, who practise some form of eastern meditation or attend Yoga classes? Over the last two decades its character has shifted from personal growth to eco-concerns and to transformation of the world.

Before we examine this new culture in the light of the values of the Gospel, we need to address two questions. Why is this phenomenon occurring at this particular time in our history: in what sense is ours a 'New' Age? Can we detect in its many manifestations an underlying foundation, a root cause?

Is it so new?

Many of the features associated with the new spirituality have existed long before our present time. Native American spirituality, I Ching, herbalism, belief in reincarnation, astrology, yoga – to mention but a few features – reach back for several millennia. Why they are being taken up again by western culture and what links them with the newer phenomena (such as the Gaia Hypothesis, Ecofeminism, Homeopathy, psychic development, etc) is that they offer a challenge or an alternative to the dominant materialistic, patriarchal paradigm of contemporary western industrial society. They offer a way of transformation both for an individual and for our culture as a whole. It is not so much a phenomenon as a state of mind attuned to possibility, looking for a better future.

Since history was first recorded, humanity seems to have been looking forward to a Golden Age. The human being has an innate longing for an age of peace and love, of justice and plenty – a return to the metaphorical harmony of an Eden way of life. The expectation of a better future is rooted in Christian tradition and even further back to the prophet Joel: 'I will pour out my spirit on everyone, your sons and daughters will proclaim my message; your old men will have dreams and your young men will see visions' (2:28) and Jeremiah (31:23-34). Paul calls Jesus the Christ the 'new creation' and urges us to 'put on a new self' (Colossians 3:10) and the Bible closes with the promise of a New Jerusalem: the vision of 'a new heaven and a new earth' (Revelation 21).

The next evolutionary leap

It is sometimes argued that while every period of history has felt itself to be on the verge of something new, it is only in retrospect that a past era can be judged to have been a turning point in the path of humanity. However, our present visionaries are convinced that what is happening in our own time is more than an improvement in our human condition: it is, as they call it, a 'quantum leap', the next evolutionary step. That humanity is on the point of a great leap forward has been the conviction of a growing number of Christian authors, from Teilhard de Chardin:

> A great many internal and external portents – political and social upheaval, moral and religious unease – have caused us all to feel, more or less confusedly, that something tremendous is at present taking place in the world. *(The Future of Man. 1964)*

to Thomas Merton:

> We are living in the greatest revolution in history, a huge, spontaneous upheaval of the entire human race. *(Conjectures of a Guilty Bystander. 1966)*

to Dom Bede Griffiths:

> The world today is on the verge of a new age and a new culture... There is a general feeling today that we are at the end of an age.... *(A New Vision of Reality. 1989).*

Previous evolutionary leaps have been in the physical order: from inorganic matter to plant life to animal life to intelligent (human) life. This new step, this quantum leap, is claimed to be of another order, an evolution into a new era of consciousness. Bede Griffiths again:

> 'I feel that we are on the eve of a new breakthrough in consciousness, of a new wave of civilisation'. *(Unpublished letter to H.W. December 22nd 1972)*

That word 'consciousness' is key to what the new spiritual trend is all about.

Some current trends

Clues to the unfolding of a new consciousness can be identified in some other current trends in society. There are signs of an increased appreciation of the dignity and worth of the human person. Witness the campaigns for justice and peace, the abolition of apartheid, concern to write off the insupportable debt owed by the poorest countries to the richest, the sense that we are all citizens of one global village.

There is the desire in all strata of society for greater participation, for democracy, for an active voice in deciding our future and the kind of world we want for our children. People are becoming less willing to have their lives manipulated by the few at the top, less inclined to be told what to do unless they feel persuaded that it is for their own or for the common good; less inclined even to be told what to believe, unless it makes sense to them, unless it is what they would call 'authentic'.

We notice that among scientists, who for generations have discounted anything spiritual or mystical, there are some who are now beginning to recognise that matter cannot be divorced from spirit, that there is a spiritual dimension to everything which, while impossible to put to objective and scientific measurement, can no longer be ignored as having an influence on physical phenomena. The theories of Relativity and Quantum Physics have pointed them in the direction of the interconnectedness of all things. Their search for the Theory of the Unified Field as the ultimate explanation of all physical reality is a case in point. Another trend towards wholeness is the greater concern today for healing as a process which should take all elements of life into account – the physical, the spiritual, the environmental, the past as well as the present – as opposed to the practice of curing which treats each disease or sickness in isolation as a mechanic might repair simply this or that damaged part of a machine.

The underlying foundation

Is there something that underlies these very diverse manifestations which is causing a change of the human paradigm? (The word 'paradigm' is used to mean the mental framework, created by the sum of our knowledge, experience, feelings, beliefs, out of which we act and which provides us with meaning, with a basis for our judgements.) There are, I believe, two factors. The first, the enormous expansion of (scientific) knowledge in our generation in both micro and macro directions, and the technology we have developed allowing us to influence infinitely more aspects of life and our environment, from genetic engineering to destroying our very planet, giving us a dangerous sense of power over creation in areas which had hitherto been perceived as the realm of God.

When new advances are made in science – particularly in those branches which affect human beings' personal lives – the warning sounds: 'Beware! We are playing God'. It is a warning that we are stepping over a boundary line that is supposed to exist between what human beings are permitted (by God, presumably) to achieve through our own efforts and what can only be achieved (at least until now) by God. But who draws this line? Who, if not God, is to decide what is human business and what is God's business? And if it be God who draws the line, how do we know where it lies?

Whatever further steps we take to promote our future evolution – wresting such powers from God, so to speak – we can be certain that they must have been written into the structure of the Universe as God originally willed it, but only now are their potentialities being realised. In this sense, such steps are good rather than evil.

Playing God

To play God in the sense of utilising our God-given intelligence in order to benefit increasingly from the potential of the created world is our human destiny. But hidden in that ability is the danger of playing God in the sense of obtaining more and more control over nature for our own selfish purposes, such that a minority of people gain control over the lives of a majority. A case in point is with the present extending of the patent laws. Their original purpose was to protect mechanical inventions. Today they cover almost every commodity. Even medicinal plants, used for centuries by indigenous people, being patented by multinational drug companies for their own exclusive use and wealth. The exercise of 'God-power' must always have as motive to enable, not to control.

In our human history there have been several clear leaps across such a supposed God-human dividing line: leaps which enabled our ancestors to achieve what their forbears would hardly have dared to dream of. The first, the greatest as far as our evolution was concerned, we have already dwelt upon. The leap out of Eden: the leap from undifferentiated union towards differentiated union. The next must have been the ability to make fire. This opened up so many new possibilities for our ancestors, from clearing the bush of wild animals to the first steps in cooking food to providing warmth and so allowing the exploration of colder regions.

The next I have touched upon as well. What is called the Axial Period (approx. 600-300 BCE) when rational thinking developed and a higher consciousness was reached. From our point of view here, I would include among the contributors to this leap, though not within the historic period, the appearance among us of Jesus of Nazareth and the extraordinary effects his vision has had upon, first our western culture, and later upon world culture.

The next great 'take-over' of divine power must be with the Industrial Revolution with all its consequences, expressed in so many forms, allowing people to achieve with machinery so much that previously was physically beyond their ability. In consequence, humanity felt itself to be more self-sufficient. There was less need than previously to call upon divine intervention. There was less need of God in daily life.

I would mark August 6th 1945 as a date when we crossed further into God's domain. By exploding the first atomic bomb over Hiroshima, killing 75,000 people (and injuring tens of thousands of others) we moved from an ability to commit mass homicide to the capability of omnicide. From that moment we seized from God control of our planet. From now on it is we, not God, who decide whether to maintain it in its evolutionary journey or whether to destroy it all with one mighty explosion. We are in charge: not God.

And today we are again crossing over the boundary into God's territory with our experiments into genetic engineering. Coming generations are no longer to be born at God's Will but will be planned and designed when and how we want them.

Each threshold crossed faces us with new moral problems to address for which there are no given guidelines. We have to make our own decisions with as broad a perspective as we are able. Are we 'playing God'? Yes. Why not? We claim for ourselves that we are made in the image of a creating God. The world and its evolution is no longer thought of as depending upon God. The human species is now responsible for making the world's and our own history.

Children have so much to teach us. They are curious about what is beyond. They are inventive. They take risks. They display enthusiasm. Enthusiasm literally means 'the God within' (en-theos). To be enthusiastic is to exercise God's creative energy within us.

Multiple choice

I believe the second factor causing a change in the human paradigm is our affluence which has turned us into a 'choice' society. This leads to a pick-and-mix attitude to life-styles, to values and to beliefs. It has brought people to 'own' their spirituality: to map out their own spiritual journey and not to be afraid of setting aside beliefs and practices they feel are no longer helpful.*

These two characteristics (the expansion of knowledge and the variety of choice) mark an evolution of human consciousness, a fundamentally new way of understanding the world around us (a new cosmology) with a consequent change in what motivates our human behaviour.

New orientations

Until recently, as we saw in Chapter 8, our western culture has caused us to see ourselves as standing outside nature, from which vantage point we, as superior beings, observed, dominated and exploited it. Now we are feeling ourselves to be an integral part of nature, of which the life-force is essentially one, though appearing in millions of different forms, in consequence of which what affects one part of

---

* From the Greek word meaning 'choice' comes the word 'heresy'. It is used in the New Testament to refer to those who have the audacity to choose their own way of life in contrast with the way of the majority.

creation in some way affects all others. This is the foundation of our current concern about the environment and the health of our planet.

We notice an increasing number of people concerned more for the quality of their lives than for the quantity of their possessions. People are being attracted to a more simple life-style.

People are feeling drawn more towards what is natural than what is artificial or synthetic: towards organically produced food, without additives, preferring rural to urban life and a home-based job rather than the daily commuting or being tied to nine-to-five working hours.

There is also the drawing closer of the two disciplines of science and theology, recognising that each has a contribution to make to the other. Within the Christian context we witness the steps being taken towards the unity of all Christians – the ecumenical movement – as well as the opening for dialogue between the great religions of the world.

All these signs of a growing unity are evidence of the change taking place from regarding the world as a machine (in which the whole equals the sum of the parts) to regarding the world as an organism (in which the whole is greater than the sum of the parts). The 'mechanical' world view which has held sway since Descartes (17th century) and served our ancestors well, is no longer adequate for our times. Consciously or unconsciously, we are all caught up in the pursuit of a more united world, a more harmonious way of life; a movement towards wholeness, interrelatedness, non-dualism, inclusiveness. This shift of consciousness could be regarded as the dynamic of the current spiritual trend. In a word, we are being caused to change our foundational story (or, in New-Age-speak, to create a new 'meta-narrative') from which we derive the visions and values that form our culture.

A Christian response

How does this new scene mesh with our Christian narrative? While moves towards unity and harmony are pointing us in a Kingdom-of-God direction, can we say that all its manifestations are equally welcome?

We have already said that the kernel of Jesus' Good News was about the Kingdom of God. The 'Kingdom' was the metaphor Jesus employed to reveal to us 'God's secret plan he had already decided to complete by means of the Christ' (Ephesians 1:9): The God design for creation. What is this design? What is the destiny of our world? For the Christian it is described in the Letter to the Ephesians: 'This plan, which God will complete when the time is right, is to bring all creation together, everything in the heavens and on Earth, with Christ as head' (1:10).

To make the Jesus vision a reality in our present day we have constantly to be reading 'the signs of the times'. This expression, in its Biblical sense, means to recognise in significant events and contemporary trends those areas in which we can see divine evolutionary energy at work bringing about its purpose and conversely, to recognise those areas of life which we judge to be militating against it: what we call the sinful situations.

This then is the measure that believers in Jesus of Nazareth must hold up to present trends in spirituality with their various manifestations in order to decide whether they are to be given our support and encouragement or whether to be opposed. Let us return to their main characteristics.

A kingdom judgement

Concern for the quality of life, rather than for the quantity of possessions, is surely a Gospel attitude to life, provided that our concern for quality is not limited to the physical but includes the spiritual dimension of life. This it seems to do in the quest for the experience of wholeness of body, mind and spirit, the three dimensions of our humanity (I Thessalonians 5:23).

A sign of the awareness of our interconnectedness – the basis of the practice of compassion – is the growth of different forms of communes, intentional (basic) communities and networks. It is estimated that there are over five hundred of these in Britain alone that have a Christian motivation, excluding those of Religious

Congregations. They have been described as the modern equivalent of the medieval monastery, standing apart from mainstream society, modelling a new way of living Gospel values.

Even the author of the Letter to the Ephesians, recognises a movement towards unity, not only among all of humanity with Christ as head, but a cosmic unity of the whole of creation, of 'everything in the heavens and on Earth'. (Of course the author was writing with a very simplified cosmology of a saucer-shaped Earth with a Heaven above and Sheol below, unaware of the vastness of the Universe.)

The sense of the inter-relatedness of all things includes creation's relationship with the Creator. While the stress of Scripture and Church tradition has been on the transcendence of God, (God out there, beyond the Universe) the emerging new consciousness is laying more stress (but not exclusively) on the immanence of the Divine: God's energising presence in every atom of the Universe. This, as we said, is what some theologians today are referring to as panentheism: God *in* all and all *in* God.

While the central theme of Jesus' Good News was in terms of the Kingdom of God, the core of that announcement was on right relating, with God and with each other. What inspires our right relationships is the ability to recognise the presence of the Divine in everyone, a characteristic of the life of Jesus. And one can add, our need to have a right relationship to and respect for our environment on account of recognising the presence of Divine energy activating all creation.

In this time of transformation, a time when all the cultures of the world are converging, we are discovering the values of the paths towards the Ultimate Unity pursued by other Faiths. Among the spiritual practices reaching the West from the East in recent decades is that of deep meditation. This has caused us to delve into our own spiritual history and rediscover there meditative practices long since neglected in the western Church.

Although the brevity of this chapter does not allow a fuller treatment of all the phenomena associated with the new spirituality, contemplative meditation, as one of them, does require special mention not only because it is becoming increasingly popular in the West, but because such meditation techniques that enable the mind to transcend are regarded as one of the chief means to bring about the new era of consciousness. So we will devote the next chapter to this subject.

Our spiritual task

What falls under the umbrella of the trends of contemporary spirituality is vastly more than a number of fringe activities and questionable practices. It is an evolving human consciousness which is providing us with a new form of understanding and a new way of evaluating our lives and our place in the Universe.

Thomas Berry, the American theologian who describes himself as an historian of cultures, a 'geologian', sums up his understanding of this culture in these words:

> What is clear is that the Earth is mandating that the human community assume a responsibility never assigned to any previous generation. The human community is passing from its stage of childhood into its adult stage of life. We are being asked to accept responsibility commensurate with our greater knowledge. We are being asked to learn a new mode of conduct and discipline. This is pre-eminently a religious and spiritual task, for only religious forces can move human consciousness at the depth needed. Only religious forces can sustain the needed effort. Only religion can measure the magnitude of what we are about... Our task at this critical moment is to awaken the energies needed to create the new world, to evoke a universal communion of all parts of life. (*The Dream of the Earth*)

Our discernment

We can classify the elements of the 'New Age' phenomenon into three groups. There are those which promote unity, drawing all things together 'with Christ as head', even if not acknowledged in those terms. These are clearly to be encouraged and participated in by the Christian who is able to interpret them as signs of the Jesus vision being lived.

Then there are, what we might term, morally neutral elements. Their value in furthering the Kingdom depends upon our motive in using them and this is enlivened by our faith. Falling into this category would be such as yoga, reflexology and other forms of complementary medicine, sacred circle dance, green values, eco-feminism and technological communication.

Thirdly, there are elements which the Christian must reject and oppose because their values are antagonistic to the Jesus vision. Among these are the activities which cause disintegration; those which promote self-development at the expense of the common good; those which prevent growth in any form – personal, inter-personal or the full flowering of our planet; those which ignore the place of suffering, the shadow side of human life; those which deny the Transcendent as the source of all life, all goodness; those clearly which employ a power which is destructive.

A rule of thumb to discern the Christian value of these 'New Age' characteristics is to ask oneself: Is it life-enhancing? Jesus told us to base our judgement upon the fruits. He did not say upon the roots!

The new spirituality presents a challenge to Christians to re-express the core of the Good News in terms which are meaningful and appeal to our society today. We have to announce the vision and values we stand for in the language of today's spiritual seekers. The beliefs of our Faith have to be re-stated and explained within the paradigm of the new cosmology, the current scientific understanding of the origin and destiny of our Universe.* Failure in this will simply fossilise Jesus' Good News in a form appealing more to historians than to those who search today to give meaning to their lives.

---

* An attempt at this is found in my book: *Tomorrow's Faith: A New Framework for Christian Belief.*

11 A key to bring the vision to reality

A S a small boy during World War II I was sent each Summer holiday to stay with two maiden aunts in a mid-England village, to escape the London bombing raids. These aunts owned a walled garden in which they grew a large variety of fruit and vegetables to supplement the food rations. Being some distance from their cottage, the door into this plentiful world was kept locked with a great padlock, to deter the village lads from stealing. Each day I would be sent up the road to collect what was needed from this garden. To hold in my hand the key to the great lock made me feel very important. So small an object, it was the one thing that could open the big wooden door to let me enter another world: a world of fresh smells and tastes and the song of birds which I never experienced in London. I held the key to a wonder world.

There exists such a key, already within everyone's grasp, which enables us to bring about, in our own lives and in our own surroundings, that wonder world which was the creative vision of Jesus.

The key lies in the word 'meditation'. The practice of meditation enables us to reach beyond our everyday selves and enter our deeper selves where we can experience the presence of the Divine, the source of the energy that empowers us to make the Kingdom vision a reality in our lives. We have already seen (Chapter 2) the role that meditation must have played in the life of Jesus.

What is meditation?

The actual word 'meditation' can lead to confusion because in western and eastern cultures the word is used quite differently. So misunderstanding arises when we in the West understand eastern meditation in our western way.

In our part of the world, before the 1960s, the word 'meditation' was used almost exclusively in a religious context. It was understood to mean a manner of praying. It is still used this way in Church circles and by writers of spiritual books, which is why many Church members have problems with forms of meditation coming to us from the East.

Religious writers and preachers in the West use the word 'meditation' to describe an exercise of the mind whereby we reflect upon some religious truth – often pondering a text from the Bible or the words of a prayer – consciously in the presence of God. This is one way of praying. Another way, described in religious books in our culture, is called 'the prayer of quiet' or 'contemplation'. By this is meant a state of active passivity in which no words are used or thoughts dwelt upon, but rather it is an awareness of God's presence during which the praying person is open to the inspiration of the Holy Spirit in his or her depth. We use the word 'contemplate' in a non-religious context when we speak about contemplating a sunset or the night sky or when we are moved by a piece of music. Each is a non-verbal, non-thinking experience which touches us deeply.

Eastern spiritual writers use the two words 'meditation' and 'contemplation' just the other way about!

Here we are using the word in its eastern sense, which is now becoming the more popular understanding in the West, especially among non-Church people. So when we speak of meditation today we are describing an exercise which is not purely religious but is a natural human means to enable the mind to reach deeper levels of consciousness than we usually experience in our daily life. It is an ancient art which pre-dates all the major religions.

To say that meditation is not purely religious is not, however, to preclude the fact that it does have a spiritual dimension. That is to say, the entry into transcendental consciousness brings about a growth in our wholeness: it unifies our body, mind and spirit by putting us in touch with the centre of our being. And the centre of our being is the point at which the Divine touches us. For this reason, people who have started to meditate for purely physical reasons (to reduce their blood pressure, to lower their stress level) or mental reasons (to enhance their creativity, to improve their memory) begin to find, after a time, that they are undergoing a spiritual awakening, maybe even leading to a wide range of spiritual experiences. The enrichment to the areas of mind, body, behaviour and environment, which meditation brings about, cannot be separated from – still less be in opposition to – the enrichment of the spiritual dimension.

Why is meditation a key?

The practice is a key which opens up exciting new possibilities enabling us to live more fully.

The benefit of meditation is both personal and social. Together, the effect is to develop more harmonious relationships – with self, with others, with the Universe and with the Transcendent – all qualities of Kingdom living which we have been considering in previous chapters. First, we will deal with the benefits to us personally.

The personal benefit

From our earliest days each of us has been trying to discover our true identity. At first unconsciously, and as we grew into adolescence, more consciously. We have been trying to find the answer to the question: Who am I?

Even before we were at an age when we were able to ask the question consciously, we had started to build up a Self which we wished to project. We did this first by imitating people we admired or people close to us. We tried to present an image of ourselves that we wanted people to notice, to admire, to love. In so far as the ingredients of this Self came from outside us, were imitations of other people, we were building up a false, unreal Self. The real Self, our true identity, is born from within our own depth.

A traditional Christian expresses this by saying that when God created each one of us He had a unique person in mind, like no other among the six and a half billion people presently populating the Earth. Our life's work is to grow in knowledge of who that person really is and to take the means to become that person, the fully human person, that God intends each of us to become. In other words, our real Self.

Sadly, all of us spend a great deal of energy trying to give reality to our unreal Self, which is no more than the facade we wish to project, the sham hero we want people to admire or the suit of armour we defensively wear lest people discover our vulnerability. We waste so much of our time with the concerns of that world which stimulates and reinforces our false Self. If we think for a moment about some of our acquaintances, we have to say of a few of them: After all these years I have never met the real John Bloggs. He has only let me meet him at surface level.

The false Self battles to dominate the true Self. It divides us in two: prevents us from being whole. The source of our wholeness, in which body, mind and spirit are in harmony, is the real Self because the unifying power comes from within the depth of our being. Christians are taught from childhood that God's will for them is that they should be holy. The word 'holy' can send a shiver down the spine of some people. It conjures up pictures of simpering sugary saints. In fact that word 'holy' comes from the same root as 'whole'. A truly holy person is one who has grown into the real integrated Self whom God intended her to become, and inevitably in doing so has grown into a close relationship with God, the source of each person's reality. The real Self is able to acknowledge and accept her faults and weaknesses as much as being able to acknowledge and accept her strengths and gifts. This is true humility: to live as the reality we were created to be.

To become an integrated, real, whole person can take a lifetime – and some never become it this side of death. In the passage of death is the final letting go. Letting go not only of all our possessions, but of all falsehoods, all pretence. That final letting go is less agonising if we have begun it already during life. The process is like peeling off the layers and layers of an onion until one comes to the core at the centre.

The way to wholeness

One of the characteristics of our times is that the pragmatic, rational, experimental world of the scientist is drawing nearer to the experiential, transcendent world of the mystic. Ever since the birth of modern science in the 17th century the two ways of understanding our world have been along very different paths.

Western science has, until well into the 20th century, offered a very mechanistic world view: that the world and all within it – including our human bodies – is made up of parts. We notice the application of this principle most obviously in the science of medicine. When a part of the body is unwell a medicine is prescribed to cure that particular part, just as when a machine breaks down the faulty part is repaired.

The shift today is towards understanding our world as a living organism and all that goes to make it up – ourselves included – as part of that organism. We form part of a whole where the whole is greater than the sum of its parts. In the medical field doctors are now appreciating that to maintain health it is not enough to cure one ailing part of the body but are taking into account the total life of the person: their environment, their relationships, their eating habits, their family medical history and those things in their daily round which cause them stress.

All the great spiritual masters of East and West have always taught that life is essentially one. Deep within all of us is a desire for wholeness – a God-given desire.

This innate desire is now manifesting itself in our everyday lives in the West. Children are being taught to be co-operative rather than competitive, we take means to eat a better balanced diet, we are more concerned about our relationship with the environment, we feel a responsibility to give aid to the victims of disaster at the other side of the globe because these people share our humanity, we have an increasing sense of all being part of one Earth.

This growing awareness, this increasing attraction towards wholeness is a sign of the level of consciousness which is evolving in humanity today. For Christians, this move towards unity should come as no surprise. The Letter to the Ephesians describes God's great design for His creation as a journey towards that same unity with the Divine that Jesus experienced (Ephesians 1:8-10).

A gift from the East

Eastern forms of meditation, such as reciting a mantra, have come to us in the West today as a particularly important gift which we can exercise to sharpen our awareness of the source of all life. One important aspect of the gift is that it has caused us to reflect upon our own mystical tradition in the West and to become aware that already in the 4th century in Egypt John Cassian was teaching mantric prayer. So was the anonymous English author of *The Cloud of Unknowing* in the 14th century. In the Eastern Orthodox Church the mantra we call the 'Jesus Prayer' has been a practice as far back as we can recall.

The practice of meditation unfolds higher states of consciousness which cause a change in our perception of things, inviting us to respond accordingly. Our senses become more attuned to the rhythm of the Universe and we experience a growing harmony, peace and oneness within ourselves and all around us.

However, it must be emphasized that the transcendence brought about by meditation does not actually create the wholeness we describe: its seed is already within us though we are largely unaware of its existence. What meditation does is to nourish this seed and so produce in us an awareness that enables us to experience and comprehend life in its real nature as a whole and as having its source in the Godhead.

For many people, their first weeks and months of following

a regular meditation discipline may result in dramatic spiritual experiences because they are discovering this new dimension which was for long hidden in their lives. Some have found that their practice brings about a deeper awareness of and appreciation for the Word of God in the Bible, for the beliefs of their Faith and for the meaning of the Sacraments. A few may even have what they might describe as an experience of mystical phenomena. It is important to recognize that these are happening purely at the psychological level. All spiritual writers say they should be ignored, certainly not encouraged. They may result from a sudden and extreme release of stress. They are no indication of sanctity nor are they a measure of our spiritual growth. The great Christian mystics teach that spiritual growth is a gift of God and develops through a growing relationship with God and an awareness of His presence in our depth. It is not something we can produce by our own effort. We can only open ourselves to God's Spirit acting in our depth. The contrary is equally true: days and months of seeming aridity and lack of 'progress' in meditation is not a sign of God's withdrawal. The saints often describe this experience as the dark night of the soul. It is a time when we can be tested as to whether we seek the God of gifts or only the gifts of God.

The social dimension of meditation

The accusing finger is sometimes pointed at the meditator as someone who seeks flight from reality: as one who is concerned only with his personal development. Meditating has been called an ego-trip.

While personal benefit might be the motivation that attracts some people to it, the effect it produces is infinitely wider.

There is a social dimension to the practice of meditation which operates at two levels. One is at the affective level. Metaphorically speaking, it allows the heart to expand. The practice causes us to become more open, more loving, more compassionate in proportion as we are gradually becoming more whole. In fact we have an increasing experience of entering into, of being one with, the oneness of all humanity. Because it is an experience, this effect is difficult to describe. But it could be said that we increasingly feel that our own essential being is part of the very essence of humanity, so that other people's sadness becomes our own, their joy is our own joy – at a very deep level.

The other social effect is at the scientific level: the influence of meditation on the field of consciousness.

Our great-grandfathers knew nothing about radio waves until an inventor, Marconi, demonstrated a way in which the human voice could be sent from one box, the transmitter, to another, the receiver, at a distance beyond the natural range of the human voice. And there was no connection between the boxes: the transmission was wireless. Nowadays every household benefits from this discovery without a thought, in its use of radio, television and even satellite. Today we are discovering something further: the effect of waves of energy sent out by the human mind. Our brains are like radio transmitters and receivers and, as with these instruments, the more finely the mind can be tuned, by passing into deeper states of consciousness, the greater the potential for having an effect on the surroundings. This effect has been abundantly researched in regard to one practice: Transcendental Meditation.

It has been observed that when a number of people in a given area regularly practise meditation they influence the field of consciousness in that area in such a way that there is a decrease of stress. Scientific studies made by independent researchers over the last decades in cities throughout the world have discovered that when as few as 1% of the population of these cities practise meditation the decrease in stress becomes manifest in such measurable phenomena as a drop in the number of accidents and traffic fatalities, a lowering of the crime rate, less violence, a fall in the number of hospital admissions.

When people meditate as a group, the result is even more striking. The effect can be compared with that of a platoon of soldiers marching over a suspension bridge. Thirty separate individuals crossing the bridge will cause no measurable effect. But the same number of soldiers marching across in step will cause the bridge to start swinging. The physical effect of the rhythm they produce when in step is far greater than that of their total foot power.

A group of meditators is releasing into the population's nervous system the creative energy and purification needed to throw off the inhibiting effects of self-centredness, of the unreal Self. Greater tenderness, love and understanding, sensitivity and awareness, forgiveness and generosity – all of which are social values – then follow naturally for the benefit, not only of the meditators, but for all around. Its fruit is to reduce negativity and stress in the collective consciousness.

In this respect, the Christian who practises a discipline of regular meditation – ideally twice daily – is enabled to fulfil the mission of a follower of Jesus: to manifest the existence of, and make a reality, his vision of a world of justice, love and peace.

A deeper relationship with the transcendent

When meditation is regarded as prayer we can understand how the practice contributes to a deepening of our relationship with God.

Put simply, what Christians regard as prayer is conscious communication with God. This means much more than speaking to God, asking God to supply our needs, or even giving praise to God as we do in public worship. There is a much deeper level of prayer than this: it is to be aware that we live in the presence of God: that God is present at the very centre of our being. This more profound form of prayer – which in our western vocabulary is referred to as contemplation – has been called by the mystics the Prayer of Quiet: a form of silent prayerfulness in which no words are needed, but nevertheless being actively attentive to God's presence in the depth of our being. It is not unlike the wordless communication that takes place between a mother and her baby in which they both gaze at each other in silence and in love. In prayer, we are aware with love of the divine presence at the still point of our existence. Meditation enables the mind to contact this deepest centre of our being. When that journey is made by a person who believes that it is God who is found and who is active at that deepest centre, then her meditation is indeed prayer, the very purest form of prayer. William Johnston, a Jesuit, says in his book on meditation, *Silent Music*, 'What makes meditation religious or non-religious is one's sense of values and one's motivation'. In other words, what makes a Christian's practice of any method of meditation a form of prayer is to have the desire to enter into that deepest form of communication with God.

Use the key – start to meditate

No one can teach you to meditate, just as no one can teach you to pray. All another person can do is to set the stage, show you ways, techniques to still the mind. All methods have the same purpose: to still the mind. Meditation then just happens.

The fundamental rule is: 'Don't try'. Do not look for or even expect 'results'. There are those who take up meditation because they seek enlightenment. We may all desire that but we cannot produce it to order, we cannot earn it. It is a gift, a grace. We can do no more than set up the circumstances in which it is more likely to happen. We can only prepare ourselves to become 'enlightenment-prone'! What will happen will just happen...in time. All that is required on our part is the discipline to meditate regularly, preferably each morning and evening.

As a glance along the Body-Mind-Spirit shelves of any bookshop will show, there are many different methods and techniques available today for entering into meditation. One cannot objectively say that one is better, more easy, more effective than any other. Once you have found a way with which you feel comfortable, the important thing is to stick with it. Avoid flitting from one method to another like a bee going from flower to flower searching for pollen.

Love, the fruit of meditation

As we have seen in previous chapters, the Kingdom symbol of Jesus' preaching is about fullness of life. 'I have come in order that you might have life – life in all its fullness' (John 10:10). Meditation is one way that enables us to become more fully alive: to draw on the God-source of life. This is why meditation can be described as 'a key to the Kingdom of God'.

The kernel of Jesus' Kingdom message is that we are invited into a new, non-mediated and intimate relationship with the Divine. We cannot accept this invitation to such an intimacy without also accepting an unconditional relationship with our brothers and sisters. And there's the rub!

So it becomes clear why the ultimate virtue is Love. Our being loved and our loving is our entry point into a relationship with a trinitarian, relational God. If the test of our spiritual growth is love, we have to ask ourselves whether our practice of meditation makes us more altruistic or more turned in upon ourselves. To be spiritual is to be loving.

Meditation, as I have described it, is the key to becoming a mystic. We should not think of a mystic as someone who spends hours in a trance or is the recipient of the stigmata. A mystic is someone who sees below the surface to the essence, whose vision is beyond what seems real to Reality itself, a person whose perspective is as wide as it is deep, who sees differently. Jesus was a mystic. Each of us is called to be a mystic.

> 'The Christian of the future, will either be a mystic, one who has experienced something, or will cease to be anything at all.' (Karl Rahner, *Theological Investigations. Vol.7 1971*)

The regular practice of meditation is the key we possess to open ourselves to the creative energy of God. We become empowered to be co-creators of the world that we believe God wishes it to be. Jesus called his vision of it the 'Kingdom of God'. St Paul describes it as a Kingdom of right-relating, peace and joy (Romans 14:17). How would we describe our vision of it? 'Without a vision, the people perish' (Proverbs 29:18).

APPENDIX

Thoughts to ponder

1. Do I acknowledge my ability to be creative?

2. How has my creativity manifested itself?

3. Is my life driven by a vision, an ideal? Try to formulate it in a few words.

4. How do I discern whether my vision is from a higher source or from my ego?

5. How can I communicate my vision to others?

6. Would others notice that my life is inspired, driven by a vision?

7. How do I pass on to others a vision to which I have given birth?

8. To what extent am I able to merge it with the vision of others and so empower them and myself?

9. What practical steps am I taking to make my vision become a reality; to move from ideas to action?

10. What is involved in maintaining it, keeping the energy alive?

References

Bancroft, Anne. *The Luminous Vision*, George Allen & Unwin, London. 1982

Berry, Thomas. *The Dream of the Earth*, Sierra Club, San Francisco, 1988

Borg, Marcus J. *The God We Never Knew*, Harper, San Francisco. 1997

Geoffrey Chapman. *Catechism of the Catholic Church, The*, London. 1994

Eisler, Riane, *The Chalice and the Blade*, HarperCollins, London, 1988

Enomiya-Lassalle, Hugo. *Living in the New Consciousness*, Shambala, 1986

Griffiths, Bede. *A New Vision of Reality*, Collins, London. 1989

Johnston, William. *Silent Music*, Collins, London. 1974

Jones, Laurie Beth. *Jesus, CEO*, Hyperion, New York. 1995

Merton, Thomas. *No Man is an Island*, Hollis & Carter, London. 1955

Conjectures of a Guilty Bystander, Doubleday, USA 1966

Naisbitt, John. *Megatrends,* Warner Books, New York. 1982

Osborne, Arthur (Ed.). *The Teachings of Ramana Maharshi*, London, 1962

Robinson, John A.T. *Honest to God*, SCM Press. London. 1963

Schwarz, Walter & Dorothy. *Breaking Through*, Green Books, Devon. 1987

Smith, Adrian B. *A Reason for Living and Hoping*, St Paul's Publishing, London. 2002
Tomorrow's Faith: A New Framework for Christian Belief, John Hunt Publishing, Winchester, UK. 2005
The Christ. CANA Publications, 11 Brownlow Hill, Chandlers Ford, SO53 2EB. 2002
The God Shift, Liffey Press, Dublin. 2004

Spong, John S. *A New Christianity for a New World*, Harper San Francisco. 2002

Teillard de Chardin, Pierre, *The Future of Man*, Collins, London. 1964
Science and Christ, Collins, London. 1968

Trout, Susan. *To See Differently*, Three Roses Press, Washington DC. USA 1990

Vermes, Geza. *The Changing Faces of Jesus*, Penguine Books. 2001
Jesus the Jew. SCM Press, London. 2001

Young, Frances. *The Making of the Creeds*, SCM Press, London. 1991

Zohar, Danah & Marshall, Ian. *Spiritual Intelligence*, Bloomsbury, London. 2000

O

is a symbol of the world,
of oneness and unity. O Books
explores the many paths of wholeness and spiritual understanding which
different traditions have developed down
the ages. It aims to bring this knowledge in
accessible form, to a general readership, providing practical spirituality to today's seekers.

For the full list of over 200 titles covering:
ACADEMIC/THEOLOGY • ANGELS • ASTROLOGY/
NUMEROLOGY • BIOGRAPHY/AUTOBIOGRAPHY
• BUDDHISM/ENLIGHTENMENT • BUSINESS/LEADERSHIP/
WISDOM • CELTIC/DRUID/PAGAN • CHANNELLING
• CHRISTIANITY; EARLY • CHRISTIANITY; TRADITIONAL
• CHRISTIANITY; PROGRESSIVE • CHRISTIANITY;
DEVOTIONAL • CHILDREN'S SPIRITUALITY • CHILDREN'S
BIBLE STORIES • CHILDREN'S BOARD/NOVELTY • CREATIVE
SPIRITUALITY • CURRENT AFFAIRS/RELIGIOUS • ECONOMY/
POLITICS/SUSTAINABILITY • ENVIRONMENT/EARTH
• FICTION • GODDESS/FEMININE • HEALTH/FITNESS
• HEALING/REIKI • HINDUISM/ADVAITA/VEDANTA
• HISTORY/ARCHAEOLOGY • HOLISTIC SPIRITUALITY
• INTERFAITH/ECUMENICAL • ISLAM/SUFISM
• JUDAISM/CHRISTIANITY • MEDITATION/PRAYER
• MYSTERY/PARANORMAL • MYSTICISM • MYTHS
• POETRY • RELATIONSHIPS/LOVE • RELIGION/
PHILOSOPHY • SCHOOL TITLES • SCIENCE/
RELIGION • SELF-HELP/PSYCHOLOGY
• SPIRITUAL SEARCH • WORLD
RELIGIONS/SCRIPTURES • YOGA

**Please visit our website,
www.O-books.net**